CULTURES OF THE WORLD
Ukraine

Cavendish
Square

New York

Published in 2018 by Cavendish Square Publishing, LLC
243 5th Avenue, Suite 136, New York, NY 10016
Copyright © 2018 by Cavendish Square Publishing, LLC

Third Edition

Cataloging-in-Publication Data

Names: Bassis, Volodymyr. | Dhilawala, Sakina. | Nevins, Debbie.
Title: Ukraine / Volodymyr Bassis, Sakina Dhilawala, and Debbie Nevins.
Description: New York : Cavendish Square, 2018. | Series: Cultures of the world (third edition) | Includes index.
Identifiers: ISBN 9781502627445 (library bound) | ISBN 9781502627377 (ebook)
Subjects: LCSH: Ukraine--Juvenile literature.
Classification: LCC DK508.515 B37 2018 | DDC 947.7 --dc23

Writers, Volodymyr Bassis, Sakina Dhilawala; Debbie Nevins, third edition
Editorial Director, third edition: David McNamara
Editor, third edition: Debbie Nevins
Art Director, third edition: Amy Greenan
Designer, third edition: Jessica Nevins
Production Manager, third edition: TK
Cover Picture Researcher: TK
Picture Researcher, third edition: Jessica Nevins

PICTURE CREDITS

PRECEDING PAGE
The flag of Ukraine.

Printed in the United States of America

CONTENTS

UKRAINE TODAY

REFORM IS HAPPENING. UKRAINE IS CHANGING." THAT optimistic message is posted front and center on the Ukrainian government web portal. It's an extraordinary statement for a government to make—an acknowledgement of past failures and wrongs. For anyone familiar with Ukraine, the reference is clear. Ukrainians have little trust in their government—with good reason, considering its reputation for corruption and the alarming events of recent history.

The second part of the statement above is certainly true, though perhaps not in the way the Ukrainian government intended. Physically, Ukraine recently lost control of some of its territory to Russia—in 2014, Russia invaded Ukraine's Crimean Peninsula and claimed it as its own. Although Ukraine, the United Nations, the United States, and most of the international community continue to view Crimea as belonging to Ukraine, it seems doubtful that Russia will give up its claim.

Ukraine had a short moment of independence in 1919, but has spent most of its recent history under Russian rule. Therefore, Russia's aggression in Ukraine in the twenty-first century might stem from a certain sense of entitlement. Russian President Vladimir Putin explained he took over Crimea to protect the interests of

In January 2017, an activist in Independence Square in Kiev demands the president of Russia remove troops from Eastern Ukraine.

the ethnic Russians living there. Alternatively, he might simply have taken back what he thought of as Russia's rightful property, mainly because he could. Who or what was there to stop him?

As if losing Crimea wasn't bad enough, Ukraine has been fighting an ongoing war with Russian separatists in eastern parts of the country since 2014. At this writing, it seems possible that Russia could also take that region, despite a peace treaty negotiated in 2015 called the Minsk Agreement. Russia continues to deny involvement in the hostilities, but evidence suggests otherwise. With its powerful Russian neighbor looming, Ukraine is under a great deal of pressure.

To understand Ukraine today, it's necessary to step back and see the bigger picture. Ukraine is a big country in Eastern Europe. It borders Russia to its north and east, and the Black Sea to the south. It also borders Romania, Moldova, Hungary, Slovakia, Poland, and Belarus. Its capital Kiev (also spelled Kyiv) is located on the Dnieper River in the north central part of the country. In terms of area, Ukraine is the largest country in Europe, not counting the

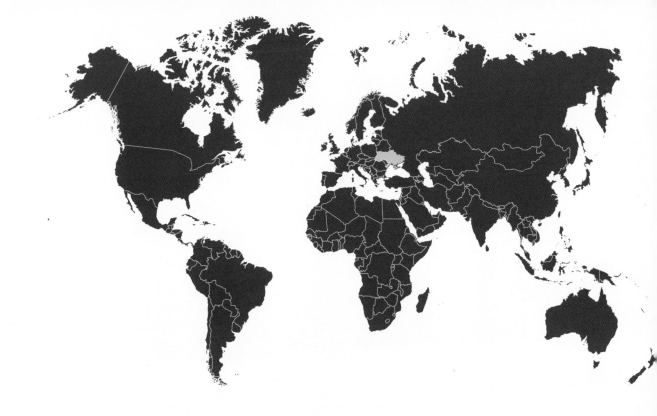

This world map shows Ukraine's size and location in Europe.

vast part of western Russia that lies in Europe. (The Russian Federation spans two continents, Europe and Asia.) But Ukraine is not the most populous country in Europe. That distinction goes to Germany—again not counting the European part of Russia—and Ukraine falls to seventh- or eighth-largest, depending on sources.

Ukraine has only been an independent country since 1991. It spent the better part of the twentieth century as a communist republic of the Union of Soviet Socialist Republics (USSR), or Soviet Union. In the nineteenth century, it was part of the Russian Empire. During those times, many people of Russian ethnicity moved into Ukraine, especially its eastern and southern regions, bringing with them their language and loyalties to the Russian homeland.

When the Soviet Union was dissolved in 1991, its fifteen republics became independent nations. Ukraine, for its part, has spent the years since then trying to figure out what kind of a nation it wants to be. Many Ukrainians want to embrace their Europeanness and model their nation after their neighbors to the west—progressive, democratic, free-market societies. Others, feeling a historic and cultural kinship with Russia, want to lean east.

Perhaps the biggest problem facing Ukraine, aside from the territorial disputes and hostilities already mentioned, is corruption. The Corruption Perceptions Index (CPI), a ranking published annually by the non-governmental organization Transparency International, generally defines corruption as "the misuse of public power for private benefit."

Bribes, cronyism (the appointment of friends and associates to positions of authority, without regard to their qualifications), embezzlement (using an organization or client's money as your own), and outright theft are rampant across many sectors of Ukrainian society. Such methods are often seen as accepted, or at least necessary, ways of doing business. According to the CPI, Ukraine is the most corrupt country in Europe, with everyone from traffic police to judges to elected officials in on the take. The court system in particular is said to be rotten to the core. Even health and education professionals—doctors and teachers!—are often guilty of demanding bribes in exchange for services.

In 2016, the CPI rated Ukraine at number 131 out of 176 in the world on a scale in which the higher number indicates a higher degree of corruption. In that year's report—in which Denmark and New Zealand shared the number one position for "cleanest," or least corrupt, Ukraine shared the 131st position with the likes of Iran, Kazakhstan, Nepal, and Russia—landing squarely in the "most corrupt" category. (For further comparison, that year the United States ranked 18, and the most corrupt countries in the world, at 174, 175, and 176, were North Korea, South Sudan, and Somalia.) With such evidence to back it up, the common claim that Ukraine is a kleptocracy, or a country run by thieves, doesn't seem to be an exaggeration.

This is not to say that average Ukrainians are thieves. Not at all. When masses of Ukrainian citizens took to the streets in the so-called Orange Revolution of 2004, and more recently in the *Euromaidan*, or Ukrainian Revolution, demonstrations of 2014, they were protesting corruption.

To say the Ukrainian people are unhappy with the corrupt state of their government and nation is not just an assumption. It's a truth borne out by yet another international rating—the World Happiness Report. This annual

evaluation, conducted by the United Nations Sustainable Development Solution Network, measures the world's happiness according to a number of national and individual variables for each country. These include gross domestic product (GDP) per capita (an economic statistic indicating standard of living); social support; life expectancy; freedom to make life choices; generosity; and—yes—the absence of corruption, or trust. For this analysis, data is collected from people in more than 150 countries. In 2017, Ukraine ranked 132 out of 155, indicating that Ukrainians are among the most unhappy people in the world.

Naturally, that doesn't mean that every individual Ukrainian person is miserable, or that people don't enjoy the ordinary pleasures of living. But it does highlight a very complex and difficult problem in a country which otherwise has a wealth of positive attributes and resources. So, when the Ukrainian government claims on its website that "reform is happening," people everywhere can only hope that's true.

Violence ensues between protesters in the street and police behind the fire barricade at the height of the Ukrainian Revolution on February 18, 2014, in Kiev.

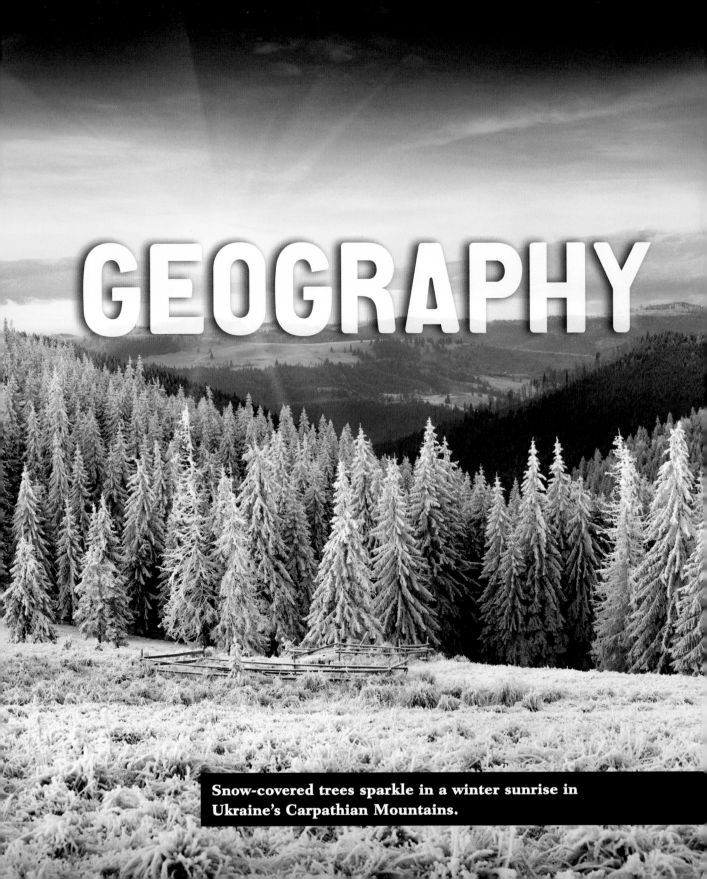

GEOGRAPHY

Snow-covered trees sparkle in a winter sunrise in Ukraine's Carpathian Mountains.

1

WHAT IS THE LARGEST SELF-contained country in Europe? It's not France, Spain, or Germany. Many people might be surprised to learn that it's Ukraine, a country in eastern Europe that borders Russia. (The part of Russia that lies on the continent of Europe is actually the largest country in Europe, but it's not the entire country.) To the north, Ukraine borders Belarus; to the northeast, Russia. To the south, it borders the Black Sea, while Romania, Moldova, Hungary, Slovakia, and Poland lie to the west.

Ukraine covers about 233,032 square miles (603,550 square kilometers) of land and water, making it just slightly larger than France, and a bit smaller than Texas. But there's a problem. Does Ukraine include the Crimea Peninsula, a major land mass on the northern coast of the Black Sea—or doesn't it? Ukraine says it does, and the United States and many nations agree (as of 2017). The numbers given here include the peninsula as part of Ukraine's total area. In 2014, however, Russia annexed Crimea and now claims it as its own. The dispute over the region has caused relations between the two nations to deteriorate.

In the past, Ukraine was often referred to in English as "the Ukraine," and older sources may still carry that style. However, since the country's independence in 1991, the preferred usage is to drop the "the," and simply use "Ukraine." Most media sources have adopted the newer style. The same approach holds true for Crimea, which is discussed in this chapter.

Haystacks dot the fields in a farming village on the outskirts of the Carpathian Mountains.

GEOGRAPHICAL REGIONS

Geographically, Ukraine is divided roughly diagonally into two major land regions. The northwestern zone is characterized by deciduous or mixed forest vegetation with a moist and cooler climate. The southeastern zone of the country is drier than the rest, with a predominantly continental climate and steppe vegetation. More than 70 percent of Ukraine's total land area is used for general agricultural purposes. During the last glacial period, the entire country was covered with a layer of loamy loess, which is the basis of the thick, black, fertile soil throughout the country.

RIVERS

Several rivers carve their paths through the Carpathian Mountains in the west, including the Tisza, the Cheremosh, the Stryi, and the Dniester. The Dniester River is one of the fastest flowing rivers in Europe, running for 876 miles (1,409 km), almost entirely in Ukraine, before it empties into the

Black Sea. The Dnieper River follows nearly the same route in the east. It is the longest river in Ukraine, running south from its source in Russia for 1,420 miles (2,285 km) until it, too, reaches the Black Sea, near the city of Kherson. The Dnieper is to Ukraine what the Nile and Amazon Rivers are to Egypt and Brazil. It's a crucially important waterway for passenger, tourist, and cargo travel. Its main tributaries are the Pryp'yat and Desna Rivers. The Danube River runs along the southwestern border, separating Ukraine and Romania. The Pivdennyi, or Southern Bug, is a large river that courses through central Ukraine.

An aerial view of Kiev shows bridges across the Dnieper River.

CLIMATE

Ukraine has a moderate continental climate with four distinct seasons. Its landscapes and gradual temperature changes keep the country out of the path of weather extremes like tornadoes and hurricanes.

In northern Ukraine, cooler weather with temperatures around 30 degrees Fahrenheit (−1°Celsius) and occasional snow may start as early as the middle of October and last into March. Altitude plays an important role in the Carpathian and Crimean Mountains, lowering temperatures and increasing precipitation as the land rises. In the coastal areas, the waters of the Black Sea and Sea of Azov create a definite tempering effect.

In Crimea, summer begins in early May and lasts until late September. There is little snow in winter. In the Carpathians, the climate is somewhat cooler, with a winter average of 25°F (−4°C), and warm, pleasant summers of 75°F—80°F (24°C—27°C). If the temperature gets higher than 85°F (29°C), it is considered extremely hot. Such excessive summer heat never lasts for more than a week, though. Long and comfortable springs and autumns are the most enjoyable seasons in Ukraine.

The Crimean Peninsula, or Crimea, is an almost-island that lies between the Black Sea and the Sea of Azov. It remains tethered to mainland Ukraine by the Isthmus of Perekop, a thin strip of land about 3.1–4.3 miles (5–7 km) wide. Providing the sole land access to Crimea as it does, the isthmus has been the site of many fierce battles throughout history. Aside from the isthmus, Crimea is separated from Ukraine by the Sivash ("Rotten" or "Putrid") Sea, a large system of shallow lagoons. The Sivash, in turn, is separated from the Sea of Azov to the east by a very narrow strip of land called the Arabat Spit, or Arabat Arrow. Barely more than a sandbar in places, it runs about 70 miles (112 km) long off the northeast coast of Crimea, but is only about 900 feet (0.17 miles) to 5 miles (8 km) wide.

The striped area shows Ukraine's Crimean Peninsula, now annexed by Russia.

Most of Crimea's land is relatively flat, made up of semiarid steppe or grasslands. Running along its southeastern coast are the Crimean Mountains, a relatively low range in which the tallest peak, Mt. Roman-Kosh, reaches a height of 5,069 ft (1,545 m).

The city of Simferopol is the capital of the Autonomous Republic of Crimea, as recognized by Ukraine, and has continued to function as such under Russian administration since 2014. For strategic purposes, however, Crimea's most important city is Sevastopol, located on the Black Sea on the peninsula's south-western tip. A closed city during Soviet times, it continues to serve as a base for the Russian Navy's Black Sea Fleet.

The port of Sevastopol.

The irregularly-shaped Crimean Peninsula has its own large protrusion, the Kerch Peninsula. It extends eastward toward the Russian territory of Krasnodar, nearly, but not quite touching it. Separating the two is the Kerch Strait, a stretch of water connecting the Black Sea and the Sea of Azov. The strait is a mere 1.9–9.3 miles (3.1–15 km) wide, and up to 59 ft (18 meters) deep. The strait is narrow enough that it seemingly could have been bridged long ago, and indeed, over the years there have been numerous plans and even one failed attempt (by the Soviet Union in 1944). However, the region's geographical conditions make construction a great engineering challenge. Nevertheless, since annexing Crimea in 2014, Russia immediately began building such a bridge, which is expected to open in 2018.

FLORA

Ukraine is rich with vegetation of more than thirty thousand types of plants and trees. About 30 percent of Ukraine's territory is covered by forests, meadows, and steppes. Expanses of pine and deciduous trees, such as oaks, make up much of the forests. Many varieties of flowers and herbs thrive in the forests, fields, and mountains, and many of the country's invaluable medicinal flora species are used in the preparation of important medicines.

The Crimean and Carpathian Mountains are homes to the largest number of endemic plant species in Ukraine. As is true in the other parts of the world, however, people have altered the natural landscapes and adversely affected the plant biodiversity. Still, the creation and maintenance of national parks and natural reserves have helped to conserve and protect the forests. Today there are fifteen nature and four biosphere reserves, eight national natural parks, and seventeen botanical gardens.

One of the country's oldest nature reserves is Askania-Nova, located in the vast steppelands of southern Ukraine. In 1898, the land was established as a private estate, but in 1919, during the Russian Revolution, it was seized

Long-horned cattle graze in the steppe region of Askania-Nova in Ukraine.

and eventually nationalized as part of the Soviet Union. Over the years, it was expanded to include a zoo, botanical gardens, and a research institute. In 1983, it was added to the UNESCO World Network of Biosphere Reserves.

FAUNA

Wildlife in Ukraine is typical of steppes—level, treeless prairie tracts— and forest areas. Centuries ago bears and wolves roamed the forests, but today the largest predator is the red fox, which can be seen in almost all the woodlands of the country, along with lesser numbers of wild boar and deer. Smaller animals include badgers, hares, red squirrels, and hedgehogs.

Rivers and lakes are the habitat for muskrat, otter, coypu (a semiaquatic rodent), and beaver. In the steppes, there are gophers and other small rodents. Ukraine has few snakes, although some venomous vipers are found in damp or swampy areas, as well as in burial mounds. There are also several varieties of harmless grass snakes and lizards.

The steppe eagle is one of the largest Ukrainian birds. Other birds of prey living in various regions of the country include hawks, falcons, and owls. Swallows, bluebirds, and sparrows are seen in abundance all over the country. In the past, bullfinches were common in the winter, but there are fewer now due to warmer winters and the widespread pollution of the environment. Wild and domestic pigeons are common in the cities, while in the forests there are magpies and cuckoos. Some lakes, ponds, and reed-covered riverbanks provide summer homes for a variety of ducks and geese. Pike, perch, perch-pike, crucian, gudgeon, carp, and many other freshwater fish are common in the rivers, lakes, and ponds in Ukraine.

ADMINISTRATIVE DIVISIONS

Ukraine is divided into administrative units called *oblasts* (OB-lahsts), similar to the states in the United States. An oblast is a political territory with its own borders, government, and capital, called the oblast center, from which the name of the oblast is derived. For example, the capital city of Cherkaska Oblast in central Ukraine is Cherkasy. Each oblast is divided into counties

This view shows Independence Square (Maidan Nezalezhnosti) in Kiev, the site of many historical events.

called *rayons* (rai-OHNs). There are twenty-four oblasts and one autonomous republic—Crimea. In addition, the cities of Kiev and Sevastopol each have a special administrative status. (However, since the 2014 Crimean crisis, Crimea and Sevastopol have been administrated *de facto* by the Russian Federation, which claims them as the Republic of Crimea and the federal city of Sevastopol.)

CITIES

Ukraine is generally densely populated, and there are a significant number of large cities. In fact, there are four cities with populations over one million and some thirty-two with populations over two hundred thousand. In Ukraine a city of fewer than one hundred thousand people would be described as small, and a settlement with fewer than five thousand people would not even be considered a town.

The capital of Ukraine is Kiev, with a population of approximately 2.9 million. Kiev was the center of Rus, a medieval East Slavic state. As the ancient capital of the Slavs, it still has numerous churches, monasteries, and monuments reflecting its golden age. Parliament, the president's headquarters, and the various ministries are all located in Kiev.

Other cities with populations over one million are Kharkiv, Donetsk, and Dnipropetrovsk in the east; Odessa (also spelled Odesa) in the southwest; and Lviv in the northwest. Lviv is called the "western capital" of Ukraine because during the repressive Soviet era, Ukrainian culture survived best in the western regions. The city was built by the Ukrainian king Danylo Romanovych in the thirteenth century and named for his son Lev. Because of its location near the western border, Lviv has a diverse population, architectural styles, and traditions, including Ukrainian, Polish, Jewish, Austrian, and Hungarian.

Kharkiv, the country's second-largest and main industrial city, is the location of the National Academies of Science. Surrounding the city are large deposits of iron ore and coal, which are mined and processed in Kharkiv.

Dnipropetrovsk is another important industrial city, located along the banks of the Dnieper River. It is a busy river port and railroad junction.

The main seaport in Ukraine is Odessa, on the northwestern shore of the Black Sea. It is the site of a large shipbuilding industry and is a manufacturing and trading center. People living and working in this cosmopolitan city represent more than one hundred nationalities.

INTERNET LINKS

https://www.britannica.com/place/Crimea
The *Encyclopaedia Britannica* online gives an up-to-date overview of Crimea's geography, history, and current political status.

https://www.lonelyplanet.com/ukraine
This travel site offers photos and information about the various cities and regions of Ukraine, including Crimea.

http://www.unesco.org/new/en/natural-sciences/environment/ecological-sciences/biosphere-reserves/europe-north-america/ukraine
This page on the UNESCO site lists the eight biosphere reserves in Ukraine, with links to each.

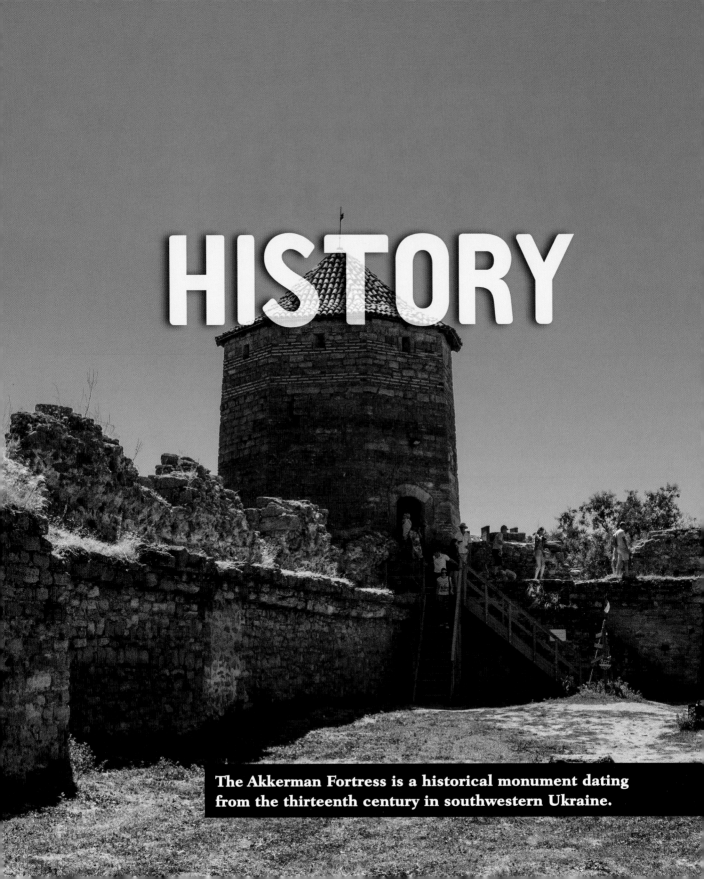

HISTORY

The Akkerman Fortress is a historical monument dating from the thirteenth century in southwestern Ukraine.

2

UKRAINE HAS BEEN AT THE crossroads of migration, trade, and war for most of its two thousand-year history. Its fertile land has attracted numerous invaders throughout its existence, and that history continues today. Since 2014, when Russia annexed Crimea, a Ukrainian peninsula in the Black Sea, Ukraine and Russia have been fighting over territory.

Ukraine spent much of the twentieth century as a reluctant part of the Soviet Union. During that time, many ethnic Russians moved into the eastern regions of Ukraine, where the Russian language is now dominant. Among many of those eastern Ukrainians, there is a lot of pro-Russian sympathy, which the government in Moscow uses to its advantage. As of 2017, fighting over Eastern Ukraine continues, and Russia appears to want to absorb the country once again. Whether Russian president Vladimir Putin will be satisfied with just Eastern Ukraine, or whether he has designs on the entire country remain to be seen.

THE EARLIEST DAYS

The first signs of people in the territory of modern Ukraine date back 150,000 years. In the late nineteenth century, excavations that took place in the village of Trypillia, not far from Kiev, uncovered evidence

Yalta, a resort city on the southern coast of Crimea, hosted the Yalta Conference in 1945. It was there that the leaders of the "Big Three" world powers–British prime minister Winston Churchill, Soviet premier Joseph Stalin, and US president Franklin Roosevelt–met to discuss the reorganization of post-World War II Europe.

Remains of the Trypillian culture can be seen in the carvings on the ancients temple wall in Busha.

of a unique civilization dating from 4500 to 2000 BCE. It soon became known as the Trypillian civilization. Trypillians lived in communities of about ten thousand people, fifteen or so individuals sharing two-story log houses, which they situated to form a large circle. Hunters and gatherers, the Trypillians also smelted bronze and produced mysteriously beautiful objects of art.

In the last millennium BCE, different groups of nomads—Cimmerians, Scythians, and Sarmatians—migrated to the southern part of modern Ukraine. The Scythians, especially, left traces of their life on the steppes near the Black Sea coasts. They were very accomplished equestrians and were among the first people to master the art of horseback riding. This mobility gave them a great advantage over their neighbors, enabling them to attack and infiltrate quickly. The Cimmerians, who still fought on foot, soon succumbed to the stronger Scythian cavalry and were forced to flee the plains north of the Black Sea. This series of victories brought great fame to the Scythians, who became very prosperous after settling in the plains. Scythian rulers were given grand burials. Grave sites discovered in Crimea and other places on the steppe have yielded tombs filled with gold and other precious metals. The Scythians enjoyed this wealth and power until the fourth century BCE, when the Sarmatians appeared on the scene. The Sarmatians ceaselessly put pressure on the Scythians, squeezing them southward until they were confined to the Crimean Peninsula. These tireless invaders gradually supplanted the Scythians as the rulers of the steppe. By the second century BCE, they had destroyed the last remnants of this once powerful community.

THE SLAVS

In the fifth and sixth centuries CE, the westward movement of the Germans stimulated the great migration of the Slavs into present-day Ukraine. They originally occupied the area between the Vistula and Dnieper Rivers, stretching northward to the Carpathian Mountains. The Slavs began to expand their region, and by the end of the eighth century they had conquered the Balkans as well. The Hungarians occupied the eastern part of the Balkan Peninsula, but they were quickly assimilated into the Slavs. Both groups converted to Christianity in the ninth century.

An Asian invasion in the ninth century divided the southern Slavs from those of the west and east. The western Slavs (Czechs, Slovaks, Elbe Slavs, Poles, and Pomeranians) adopted Roman Catholicism, while the eastern Slavs (Estonia, Latvia, Lithuania, Russians, and Ukrainians) adhered to the Greek Orthodox Church.

KIEVAN RUS

In the 400s CE, certain Slavic tribes moved south into the region. These Slavs are the direct ancestors of most modern Ukrainians. The tribes originally came from Asia, but migrated to Eastern Europe in the third or second millennium BCE.

According to ancient Byzantine historians, the Slavs were a handsome, tall, and strong people with fair hair; they were brave fighting men of great endurance, and hospitable hosts in peacetime. Their main occupation was farming. They sowed rye, wheat, barley, and millet, and traded, hunted, and fished.

The Slavs eventually made their way to the lands of present-day Ukraine, settling in the area between the Vistula and Dnieper Rivers, and northward to the Carpathian Mountain region.

Legend claims that Kiev was founded in 482 CE, (though historians say it could have been any time from the fifth to seventh centuries) by Prince Kyi, who might have been a Slavic prince of the eastern Polans tribe—if indeed he existed at all, which isn't certain. Whether the story is history or mythology, it marks the beginning of a loose federation of Slavic tribes that came to be known as Kievan Rus.

In 882, Prince Oleg of Novgorod conquered Kiev and thus began a line of rulers of the Rurik dynasty. He united numerous individual Slavic principalities to protect against aggressive Scandinavian Vikings from the north and nomads from the south. At that time the people of Kiev were known as the Rus, so the new state established by the Ruriks was called Kievan Rus.

With the city of Kiev being on the main trade route connecting the Baltic Sea with the Black Sea and the Byzantine Empire, Kievan Rus established trade with the cities of Asia and Europe—Prague, Constantinople, and Baghdad.

In 988, Grand Prince Vladimir I, the fourth member of the Rurik dynasty, joined the Eastern Orthodox Church and made Christianity the official religion of Kievan Rus. The old idols of the heathen gods were thrown into the river. Orthodox priests, who came from Constantinople, christened the Rusians, (also known as Rusyns or Ruthenians), in the water of the Dnieper River.

A monument to Rurik and Prince Oleg of Novgorod stands in Staraya Ladoga, Russia.

Kievan Rus flourished in the eleventh century during the rule of Grand Duke Yaroslav the Wise (1019—1054). It became the largest European empire—stretching from the Gulf of Finland in the northwest, to the Black Sea coast and the lower Danube in the south, and from the Carpathian Mountains in the west, to the upper Volga in the east. Foreign kings sought to establish friendly relations with Kievan Rus, and marriage was an important tool of diplomacy. Yaroslav married a Swedish princess, and married his daughters to French, Hungarian, and Norwegian kings.

After Yaroslav's death, there was a struggle for power among his three sons. The country was divided into three principalities ruled by his offspring, which made it easy prey for invaders, particularly the nomad tribes of the Polovtsy. From 1057 to 1100, Kievan Rus suffered again and again from Polovtsy invasions, which saw Kiev's decline and the end of the golden period of political stability achieved by Vladimir and carried on by his son, Yaroslav. During the same period, there was a major shift in trade routes, brought on by the First Crusade, making the route between the Baltic and Black Seas superfluous.

MONGOL INVASION

In 1223, the Mongols invaded. These armies from Mongolia, an empire in the heart of Central Asia, were led by Genghis Khan, a clever, talented, and cruel man. His armies, made up of Tatars—Turkic peoples who had themselves been conquered by and incorporated into the Mongul horde— had conquered much of Asia and now turned towards Kievan Rus and Eastern Europe. Battles raged for decades, but by the end of the 1250s, the severe rule of the Tatar Khans was established in Kievan Rus. By that time, the principalities had been at war intermittently for generations, and the Mongols' mounted warriors were too skillful for the weakened Slavs to repel.

After the defeat of the Slavs, the Mongols established a unified political system in an attempt to revive the commerce that had traditionally crossed the Central Asian plains. Although much of the country lay in ruins due to years of fighting, many cities made a surprisingly rapid recovery under the rule of the Mongols. Kiev, however, never fully regained its grandeur. Administration of the principalities was left in the hands of the Turkic leaders and Muslim merchants who had been operating in the area for generations.

In 1241 the Mongols founded the Golden Horde, a state that extended from the Danube River to the Ural River and at its height included areas such as the Crimea, Bulgaria, Moldova, and parts of Siberia. To avoid further conquest, Ukrainians moved westward and established the state of Galicia-Volhynia. The state remained independent until 1340, when it succumbed

This map shows the Galician-Volhynian Kingdom in dark green, and the extent of the Golden Horde, in yellow, in the Ukraine region.

to the superior powers of Lithuania and Poland. From the 1340s on, much of Ukraine came under the sovereignty of the Grand Duchy of Lithuania. Yet Ukrainian territories under Lithuania maintained much of their political and cultural self-determination.

In the 1380s, the Lithuanian-Polish contest for power over Galicia-Volhynia ended when Lithuania annexed Volhynia and Poland established legitimate control over Galicia. Lithuania was united with Poland in 1385 by a matrimonial union between Lithuania's Grand Duke Jogaila and Poland's Queen Jadwiga. This marriage created a dynastic union of the two powers. When Lithuania and Poland were constitutionally united by the 1569 Union of Lublin, western Ukraine and the city of Kiev came under the control of the Polish king. As Polish subjects, Ukrainians were required to learn the Polish language and to adopt Roman Catholicism, the Polish faith.

At that time there were numerous Ukrainian uprisings against their Polish and Lithuanian occupiers. Many peasants escaped from their landlords

COSSACKS

Originally runaways from unbearable living conditions under their landlords, Cossacks formed democratic military communities on the Dnieper River islands. They elected their leaders, lived a life of constant training, and fought against the Tatars, Turks, Poles, and Russians. Later, they even fought for *the Russians. Over time, numerous groups of Cossacks formed in various regions.*

They were not bound by nationality, religion, or politics. In fact, historians and anthropologists still have difficulty defining exactly who the Cossacks were. What they had in common was a fierce independence that kept them from submitting to the authority of any  *nation state, a legendary military aggressiveness, and a lifestyle that glorified raids and looting. They were Eastern Orthodox Catholics, and followed a strict internal code of righteousness.*

The group that lived mostly in the Ukraine area were the Zaporozhian Cossacks. Ukrainian history books and folk songs praise the names of prominent Cossack leaders, called hetman *(HET-mahn). Despite many attempts to disband the Cossacks, the active movement persisted until the Russian Revolution in 1917. Cossack units served mainly in the White Russian army defending the czarist Russian Empire. But the Whites ultimately lost to the Reds, the revolutionaries who went on to create the Soviet Union. Following the war, the Cossacks were heavily persecuted and their military forces fell apart.*

Since the dissolution of the Soviet Union, however, there has been a revival of the Cossack brotherhood in Russia. In 2005, Russian president Vladimir Putin officially recognized the Cossacks as a distinct ethno-cultural entity and a potent military force. In 2014, Cossack units fighting for Russia were involved in the conflict in Ukraine.

and led dangerous, but free, lives. These hardy fugitives were called *Kozaks* (koh-ZAHK), or Cossacks in English, a name that is derived from the Turkish word *qasaq* for "a free man."

SEVENTEENTH-CENTURY UKRAINE

The strong Cossack army and the system of Hetmanship brought revival to the Ukrainian people and their culture. The Cossack troops made many successful raids on Moscow and in Crimea in the early 1600s and fought with the Polish army and the Tatars. The position of the leader of the Orthodox Church, the patriarch, was restored in 1620, and the first institute for higher learning, called the Kievan Academy, was founded by Petro Mohyla in 1632.

Besides the regular raids against Poland, several anti-Polish uprisings took place in different parts of Ukraine in 1630, 1635, and 1638. One prominent Cossack leader, Bohdan Khmelnytsky, organized an anti-Polish movement that triumphed in several battles but never completely defeated the Polish army. In 1654, Khmelnytsky signed the Pereyaslav Treaty, uniting Ukraine with Russia, in an effort to oust the Poles from power. The united Cossack-Russian army was a powerful fighting force. The Cossacks soon realized, however, that while fighting one oppressor, they appeared to be falling under the thumb of another, even stronger one—Russia.

In 1708, the leader of the Cossack army, Hetman Ivan Mazepa, left the Russian army and joined Swedish King Karl XII. In the ensuing battle at Poltava, the Swedish-Cossack army was defeated by the Russians, which set the stage for the Russian colonization of Ukraine.

UKRAINE IN THE RUSSIAN EMPIRE

Peter the Great (1672—1725), the czar of Russia, ruled his empire with an iron fist. Decrees limiting Ukrainian freedom were issued from the outset. The second part of the century saw the further colonization of Ukraine, with Russia taking over former Polish and Austrian territories.

In the nineteenth century, the first signs of discontent became visible. A peasant movement for freedom began in 1813; a revolt by nobles, called

Decembrists, took place in 1825 in Kiev and Odessa; and prominent Ukrainians raised their voices to restore the rights of the Ukrainian people.

At the same time, coal deposits were first discovered in eastern Ukraine; the first sugar refineries were built in central Ukraine; the southern cities of Odessa and Mykolayiv were founded; and new universities opened their doors in Kharkiv, Kiev, and Odessa. Several magazines and newspapers were published in the Ukrainian language (despite the fact that it was forbidden) and were distributed both in Ukraine and abroad.

In 1861, under the pressure of the uprisings and the wave of dissatisfaction, serfdom was abolished. Yulian Bachynsky's article "*Ukraina Irredenta*," published in 1895, was the first public mention of Ukrainian independence.

SOVIETS TAKE POWER

Poverty and hunger was rampant throughout the Russian Empire in the early twentieth century. It fueled a growing national liberation movement in Ukraine and a developing revolutionary faction in Russia. Communist revolutionaries wanted to establish a new kind of government in Russia and plotted to overthrow the czar. The leader of the Communists, Vladimir Lenin, promised the people "peace, food, and land."

The year 1917 brought the two-part Russian Revolution—in March, the Communists overthrew the czar; and in November, the Communists seized power in Saint Petersburg and Moscow.

Meanwhile, in Ukraine, the first Ukrainian National Republic was proclaimed in Kiev by the Third Ukrainian Universal Congress. In January 1918, the Fourth Universal Congress proclaimed Ukraine independent, with sovereign borders, its own currency, a constitution, and a government. The first president of the Ukrainian National Republic, Mykhailo Hrushevsky, was elected in April 1918. Lenin's new Communist state and several other nations recognized Ukrainian independence.

The republic was short-lived, though. Civil war erupted between various factions, including those who sided with the Russian Bolsheviks (Soviets). It lasted for almost two years, during which time there were several changes of government. In December 1919, the Bolsheviks invaded Ukraine, leading

Ukraine to declare war on Russia, which was still fighting its own civil war.

Meanwhile, World War I had just ended and much of Europe was being redrawn by Allied negotiators at the Paris Peace Conference. Although Ukraine sent delegates to the conference to argue for independence, the Allies couldn't agree on what to do with Ukraine. The United States at the time favored a strong, united Russia to keep the aggressor Germany in check. In the end, Ukraine was essentially left to Russia. Although Ukrainian nationals continued to strive for an independent country, by the end of 1922, Ukraine had become a republic in the vast, newly-formed Union of Soviet Socialist Republics (USSR), or Soviet Union.

Intensive industrialization of the eastern areas of Ukraine continued over the next ten years, and strict measures were taken to reorganize agriculture. The brutal new leader of the USSR, Joseph Stalin (1878—1953), abolished private farms and ordered the creation of state-run collective farms instead. Farmers were forced to give up their land and livestock and to work as hired labor on government farms. Those who protested were arrested, executed, or sent into exile.

WORLD WAR II–GERMAN OCCUPATION

After the signing of the Molotov-Ribbentrop Pact in 1939, which banned any conflict between the USSR and Germany, both countries made vast territorial gains. The new borders were considered sovereign, but both countries were preparing for war. For Ukraine, World War II started on June 22, 1941, with the German army invading its western borders and bombing Kiev. Despite the heroic defense of the major cities, all of Ukraine was occupied by July 1942.

Some Ukrainians hailed the Germans as their liberators, but it soon became apparent that Ukraine had in no way been liberated. This was clearly seen in the not uncommon attitude of Erich Koch, the German commissioner in charge of Ukraine. In 1943, he famously said, "We are a master race, which must remember that the lowliest German worker is racially and biologically a thousand times more valuable than the population here."

THE HOLODOMAR-FAMINE IN UKRAINE

Under Stalin's new agricultural program, Ukraine was one of the first areas in the USSR to be targeted for collectivization—the forced consolidation of individual farms into large, government-owned enterprises—because it was a rich grain-producing region. Wealthy Ukrainian farmers, called kulaks *(COO-lacks)—the Soviet label for those who owned a larger than average plot of land and had hired labor—were exiled or executed. Anyone who actively resisted was also labeled a kulak and suffered a similar fate. The transition caused terrible disruptions in production, but exorbitant taxes were still demanded from the peasants.*

A drought in 1932–1933 was only one factor causing a famine in which millions died of starvation. Many historians claim the Holodomor, *as it's called in Ukraine, was primarily a man-made famine exacerbated by the Soviets' collectivization agenda and their ill-conceived policies. Some say it was deliberate genocide. Nearly seven million Ukrainians starved to death in less than two years. More*

A monument to the victims of the Holodomor stands in Kiev.

than two hundred thousand desperately hungry people were arrested for merely gleaning leftover grain from the fields, which was illegal. The Soviet government tried to prevent the world from discovering what had happened in Ukraine, officially denied any reports of it as "anti-Soviet propaganda," and rejected all offers of foreign aid.

Residents of Kiev clear rubble on Khreshchatyk Street after the Soviet Red Army liberated the city from the Nazis in the autumn of 1943.

Indeed, it was the German leader Adolf Hitler's intention to exterminate about 65 percent of the Ukrainians, and enslave the rest. The country and its resources would then be used for the benefit of Germans. Under German occupation, schools and universities in Kiev were closed, and people between the ages of fifteen and sixty were used in forced labor.

Between 1941 and 1945, approximately four million Ukrainians were killed by the Nazis, including about one million Jews. Some 2,300,000 Ukrainians were deported to Germany for slave labor. Some Ukrainians helped to hide Jews; others, however, collaborated with the Nazi occupiers.

In October 1942, the Ukrainian Resistance Army formed in Lviv. It confronted both the German and the Soviet armies in the hope of attaining Ukrainian independence. By December 1942, the Soviet army had started its counteroffensive to retake Ukraine. Not until October 1944 was Ukraine finally free from German occupation. But the country found itself once again under Soviet control.

While restoration of Ukrainian industry and agriculture began immediately after the war, the restoration of its language and culture was still many years away.

TIME OF TRANSITION

In 1985, new policies of *perestroika* (pair-a-STROY-ka, "restructuring") and *glasnost* (GLASS-nost, "openness") were introduced by the first—and who would be the last—president of the USSR, Mikhail Gorbachev. These opportunities allowed a national renaissance in Ukraine to burst out. In April 1986, the Chernobyl nuclear-plant crisis added tension to the political situation. In 1987, for the first time in many years, Ukraine celebrated a Christian event, the one thousandth anniversary of the Christianization of Ukraine.

A national democratic movement called *Rukh* ("movement" in Ukrainian) was founded in September 1989, and the authorities registered it as a legal political organization in January 1990—a significant event in a country with a one-party system. Ukrainian, rather than Russian, became the official language in October 1989. Events of a similar nature were happening all over the Soviet Union.

In August 1991, an attempt by reactionary Communists to overthrow Gorbachev prompted the majority of the republics that made up the Soviet Union to ban the Communist Party. On August 24, 1991, the Ukrainian parliament declared Ukraine independent. A national referendum took place on December 1, 1991, and an overwhelming majority (about 90 percent) of Ukrainians voted for independence.

INDEPENDENCE

The new Ukrainian government faced a tough challenge in getting out from under Russia's economic influence and ensuring civil liberties and prosperity for its citizens. A difficult economic legacy, widespread corruption, and a lack of political agreement over reform led to a decade of economic decline.

Shortly before the 2004 election, candidate Viktor Yushchenko fell seriously ill. He was flown to Vienna for treatment, and was found to have acute pancreatitis with other mysterious and unusual symptoms. Toxicologists and doctors from across Western Europe

determined that he was suffering from TCDD dioxin poisoning. This potent form of dioxin is the cancer-causing contaminant in the herbicide Agent Orange, famously used in the Vietnam War to clear brush.

Although Yushchenko was found to have the second-highest level ever measured of TCDD concentration in his blood, he eventually recovered. However, he suffered severe facial disfigurement in the aftermath, with jaundice, bloating, and pockmarks called chloracne. (See Yushchenko's before and after photos above.)

Yushchenko claimed to have been poisoned by political opponents backed by Russia. Indeed the three men suspected of involvement—including one of his own staff members, the godfather of one of his children—all fled to Russia, which refused to extradite them (return them to Ukraine to face charges).

Although Yushchenko went on to serve as Ukraine's president, the poisoning case was never solved or resolved. Russia's involvement seems certain—Russia is one of the few countries that produces the type of dioxin used in the crime—but has never been proven. The Ukraine government's failure to reveal any information relating to the case caused rumors of a cover-up, which ultimately undermined Yushchenko's popularity.

The first president of independent Ukraine was Leonid Kravchuk (1991–1994). During his term, Ukraine saw a sharp fall in industrial output and inflation ballooned. His successor, Leonid Kuchma, was equally powerless to change things. During his ten-year presidency (1994–2004), restructuring and bureaucratic reform were delayed due to greedy political and bureaucratic interests.

In the 2004 presidential election, an increasing number of Ukrainians rallied under the former prime minister, Viktor Yushchenko (b. 1954), who was challenging the current prime minister supported by Kuchma, Viktor Yanukovych (b. 1950), for the presidential office. The campaign started out with Yushchenko clearly emerging as Ukraine's most popular candidate.

Leonid Kravchuk

THE ORANGE REVOLUTION

The contest between the political parties reached a climax after Yanukovich, contrary to all opinion polls, was declared the winner. Ukrainians cried foul and poured into the streets of Kiev to overturn what they saw as a rigged election. The movement developed into a campaign of civil resistance, sit-ins, and general strikes, with thousands of protesters demonstrating daily in Kiev.

The dispute attracted international attention. The European Union and the United States backed Yushchenko, and Russia openly and heavily supported Yanukovych. In the end, the orange-clad protesters emerged victorious after the Ukrainian Supreme Court nullified the election results and ordered a rerun. This second presidential election was monitored by international observers, and, indeed, Yushchenko was the winner this time. The Orange Revolution, as it became known, ushered in a new pro-Western reform-minded government led by Viktor Yushchenko.

The Orange Revolution was a great historical event for Ukraine and all of Europe. While the concept of civil society and the right to protest was innate in Europe, it did not exist in the former Soviet republics. The Orange Revolution inspired Ukraine's youth. It also changed Ukraine's dependent relationship with Russia to one of making its own independent decisions. However, it also revealed the regional differences within the country, with most of the support for Yushchenko and the Orange movement coming from the west and north of Ukraine, while the east and south tended to side with Russia.

INSTABILITY AND BETRAYAL

As president, Yushchenko was determined to bring about radical political and economic changes. But although his government did make considerable progress on issues of freedom of the media and political freedom, efforts at confronting corruption and the socioeconomic situation were not as successful.

Partisan infighting followed, creating an atmosphere of instability that influenced the 2006 parliamentary elections. A political crisis blew up after the election when the parties struggled to form a coalition government as required by new constitutional amendments. After months of political deadlock, on August 4, President Yushchenko appointed his former rival Viktor Yanukovych as prime minister.

Yanukovych rehabilitated his shady reputation and gained enough popularity to win Ukraine's 2010 presidential election legally. As president, Yanukovych worked toward a closer relationship with the European Union (EU). Many Ukrainians agreed that leaning toward Europe—away from Russia—and becoming part of the EU would benefit them economically. Then, in November 2013, on the eve of signing an important financial agreement with the EU, Yanukovych suddenly called off the agreement. Instead, he signed a treaty and a multibillion-dollar loan agreement with Russia. Ukrainians were stunned.

THE UKRAINIAN REVOLUTION

Just as in the Orange Revolution, protesters by the hundreds of thousands took to the streets. The wave of demonstrations came to be called *Euromaidan*, after Maidan Nezalezhnosti, ("Independence Square"), the main city square in Kiev, and the site of the events. At first the protesters merely demanded closer ties with Europe, but the scope of the demonstrations soon grew into a mass campaign to remove the president from power. Yanukovych was accused of corruption, abuse of power, and violation of human rights.

Demonstrations cropped up in cities across the country and continued into January and February 2014, when events turned violent and deadly. Police and government snipers fired into crowds of demonstrators, killing about one hundred people and injuring about 570.

Meanwhile, Yanukovych fled to Russia. There he remains in exile (as of 2017), charged by Ukraine with high treason. The opposition took control of the Ukraine government, with Petro Poroshenko winning the 2014 presidential election on a pro-Western platform. One of the first things the new president did was to sign the delayed EU association accord that Yanukovych had refused.

The Euromaidan protests of 2013—2014 escalated in January—February 2014 into what has come to be called the Ukrainian Revolution.

PUTIN TAKES CRIMEA

Less than a month after the events of the Ukrainian Revolution, Russian forces seized Crimea. Pro-Russian politicians in the Crimean parliament, believing the ousting of Ukrainian president Viktor Yanukovych to be illegal, held a referendum on March 16, 2014. With a reported 83.1 percent voter turnout, the referendum result was said to be 96.77 percent vote for integration of Crimea into the Russian Federation. (Many observers both within and outside of the region doubt these figures. However, some 58 percent of Crimeans are ethnic Russians, so a majority vote of some degree is not inconceivable.)

Internationally, most countries, including the United States, Canada, and members of the European Union, viewed the referendum itself as illegal. The United Nations declared the vote invalid. Nevertheless, the Crimean parliament and the Sevastopol City Council immediately declared Crimea to have seceded from Ukraine, and requested it join the Russian Federation. On March 17, Russian president Vladimir Putin immediately claimed Crimea as a Russian state. Russian troops seized Ukraine's military bases in Crimea and Ukrainian armed forces withdrew.

On July 14, 2014, a commercial airliner crashed in eastern Ukraine, killing all 283 passengers and 15 crew members. Of those, 196 people were from the Netherlands, 42 from Malaysia, and 27 from Australia. Malaysia Airlines Flight 17 (MH17) was a regularly scheduled passenger flight which had departed Amsterdam and was on its way to Kuala Lumpur along its intended flight path. The plane passed over the disputed Donbas region of Ukraine, where intense fighting was taking place between Ukrainian armed forces and Russian-backed rebels.

Western investigators eventually determined that the plane had been shot down by a Russian surface-to-air missile fired by Ukrainian rebels. The Russian-backed separatists had requested the missile system from Russia in order to fight Ukrainian military jets. Satellite footage shows the missile system was trucked into Ukraine earlier that day and returned the same night, minus one missile.

At first, the separatists denied shooting down the plane, and Russia denied any involvement. Rebel fighters prevented investigators' access to the crash site. A year later, however, an official report by Dutch authorities confirmed that MH17 was shot down by a Russian-made missile fired from

People place flowers at the Dutch Embassy in Kiev after the crash.

eastern Ukraine. The report implicates Russian soldiers in addition to separatist fighters. Did the separatists—largely untrained in such matters—mistake the commercial airliner for a military jet, or was the attack a deliberate act of terrorism? The answer is unclear.

As of three years later, some victims' families are suing Russian President Vladimir Putin and Russia in the European Court of Human Rights. However, Russia continues to deny any involvement.

RUSSIA EYES EASTERN UKRAINE

Hostilities and Russian aggression did not end with the annexation of Crimea. In April 2014, pro-Russian separatists seized parts of Eastern Ukraine in the Donesk and Luhansk regions (together called "the Donbas"). Russian and Ukranian troops routinely exchanged fire over the border. By August, Russia began sending troops and heavy military equipment into Eastern Ukraine— essentially it was an outright invasion—resulting in an ongoing armed conflict between Ukraine and Russia. While the West condemns Russian military intervention and aggression in Ukraine, Russian President Putin justifies the incursion as "defending the Russian-speaking population in the Donbas."

INTERNET LINKS

http://www.bbc.com/news/world-europe-18010123
BBC News presents a timeline of significant events in Ukraine's history from 1917 to the present.

http://www.bbc.com/news/world-europe-27308526
"Ukraine crisis in maps" follows events in maps and photos from November 2013 to February 2015.

http://www.newsweek.com/while-trump-fiddles-putin-steps-war-ukraine-550603
This 2017 article examines Ukraine's fears of a full-scale Russian invasion.

http://origins.osu.edu/article/ukrainian-crisis-russias-long-shadow
This in-depth article explains the historical background behind today's crisis situation in Ukraine.

http://time.com/95898/wolves-hundred-ukraine-russia-cossack
Time magazine looks at the involvement of Cossack forces in Russia's aggression against Ukraine.

GOVERNMENT

The blue sky over Kiev and a golden monument to independence echo the colors of the Ukrainian flag.

3

UKRAINE IS STRUGGLING TO BE A functional democracy. Since the fall of the Soviet Union in 1991, Ukraine has worked to recreate itself as an independent republic for the second time in its long history. It is a semi-presidential (or parliamentary-presidential) republic, a form of government in which a directly elected president shares executive power with a prime minister and a government appointed by a democratically elected legislature.

This is a relatively new form of government for Ukraine. Constitutional changes instituted in 2004 following the Orange Revolution made the country into a presidential-parliamentary democracy. They introduced concepts of political coalition and coalition government, and transferred some power from the president to the parliament, the Verkhovna Rada ("Supreme Council of Ukraine").

The elections are held according to the new system of proportional vote, which means votes are allocated to the political parties rather than to individual candidates. Deputies to the parliament are elected for five-year terms instead of four, and during their terms, they are not allowed to quit the party on whose ticket they ran.

On October 1, 2010, the Constitutional Court of Ukraine declared the constitutional amendments of 2004 illegal, thereby abolishing the principle of coalition creation in the parliament. In February 2014, after the Euromaidan demonstrations, the parliament passed a law that reinstated the 2004 amendments of the constitution. Three days later, the Verkhovna Rada also terminated the powers of five judges of the Constitutional Court of Ukraine for violating their oath.

In recent years, Ukraine has grappled with big problems—partisan infighting that has destabilized the government, Russian interference in its elections, and Russian invasions and annexation of it sovereign lands. The struggle is essentially between those Ukrainians who wish to align with Europe and the West, and those who want to look to, or be a part of, Russia. It's also a struggle with Ukraine's own demons, with corruption being at the top of the list.

Ukraine's leaning toward Europe and away from the Kremlin's (Russian government's) traditional sphere of influence is a major threat to Russia. The political and economic changes in Central and Eastern Europe since 1991 have had adverse effects on Russian trade there. Despite the substantial decline in trade between Russia and Ukraine following the collapse of the Soviet Union, economic interdependence between the two countries was still strong. Russia was Ukraine's biggest importer. In addition, Russia is an important investor in Ukraine, particularly in its oil industry, with four out of the six refineries being owned by Russian companies. Also, ties with Russia are especially strong in the east where many ethnic Russians live. Many of these Ukrainians were born in Russia, have relatives in Russia, and speak and read primarily in Russian.

EXECUTIVE BRANCH

After years of living under the one-party system of the Soviet Union, it is not surprising that it was difficult for most Ukrainians to believe that they could actually influence political events. But such attitudes are gradually changing. Since independence, dozens of new parties reflecting fresh views and political beliefs have arisen to fill the void of the Communist Party.

THE PRESIDENT is the chief of state. He or she is elected by popular vote and serves a five-year term. Since June 2014, the president has been Petro Poroshenko (b. 1965). He will be eligible for a second term when his first term is up. The next presidential election will be in 2019.

The president's job is to ensure that the legislative, executive and judicial branches of government do not infringe the fundamental Law of Ukraine, as stated in the constitution. He or she is empowered to suspend the decisions of government bodies and to veto laws passed by the Verkhovna Rada in order to protect citizens' rights and freedoms.

The president protects the sovereignty and territorial integrity of Ukraine. As such, he or she is the commander-in-chief of the Armed Forces of Ukraine. In the event of an armed aggression against Ukraine, the president makes decisions on the use of the country's armed forces.

The first president of Ukraine, Leonid Kravchuk, was elected almost unanimously, since he was the chairman of the Verkhovna Rada and initiated Ukraine's independence decree in August 1991. He also supported the banning of the Communist Party, despite the fact that in Soviet Ukraine he occupied one of the top positions in the Ukrainian Communist Party.

President Petro Poroshenko took office in 2014.

THE PRIME MINISTER is the head of government. He or she is nominated by the president, confirmed by the Verkhovna Rada. Since April 2016, the prime minister has been Volodymyr Groysman (b. 1978).

The prime minister is the leader of Ukraine's executive branch of government, the Cabinet of Ministers. He or she signs decrees passed by the cabinet.

THE CABINET OF MINISTERS is commonly called the Government of Ukraine. It is a body of eighteen ministries represented by their head minister, and is headed by the prime minister. Some of the ministries include Foreign Affairs, Finance, Defense, Justice, Health, Education and Science, and the like. Since 2016, the cabinet has included the newly-established Ministry of Temporarily Occupied Territories and Internally Displaced Persons (IDPs) to address the Russian-occupied parts of Donetsk, Luhansk, and Crimea.

Members of the cabinet may not combine their official duties with other work, except teaching, scholarly, and creative activities. They are not allowed to be part of any profit-making enterprise.

LEGISLATURE

The legislative body of the nation is the Supreme Council, or Verkhovna Rada (ver-KHOV-nah RAH-dah). The Verkhovna Rada is a unicameral (one house, or one chamber) parliament that enacts decisions based on the votes of its members from various political parties.

Constitutional amendments aimed at significantly increasing parliament's power were passed in 2004 and came into force on January 1, 2006. Under

The Ukrainian parliament votes for the new Cabinet of Ministers in April 2016.

the amended constitution, parliament's term was increased from four to five years, and the prime minister is nominated as head of the executive branch through a parliamentary majority. The prime minister nominates members of his cabinet, who have to be approved by parliament. The president, who formerly appointed the government and had the right to dismiss ministers, now has only the right to propose the ministers for foreign affairs and defense.

Under the amended constitution, the Verkhovna Rada now has 450 members who are elected according to the proportional representation system. Previously, under the mixed system, 225 members were elected from single-member constituencies and the remaining 225 seats were filled using a proportional system. (However, since the Russian annexation of Crimea and the partial occupation of Ukraine's two eastern provinces, 27 of the 450 seats remain unfilled.) The Verkhovna Rada initiates legislation, ratifies international agreements, and approves the budget.

The most recent parliamentary elections were held in October 2014 and the next ones are scheduled for the fall of 2019.

JUDICIARY

The Supreme Court of Ukraine is the country's highest court. It consists of ninety-five judges organized into civil, criminal, commercial, and administrative chambers, as well as a military panel. A separate Constitutional Court is made up of eighteen justices.

Since independence, Ukraine has struggled with corruption at a variety of governmental levels. Ukraine's judiciary was allegedly tainted by corruption, with judges operating in collusion with political operatives. For a judicial system to operate correctly, the justices must be free of political or commercial pressures or incentives. In 2016, the Verkhovna Rada adopted amendments to the country's constitution designed to address these concerns. The amendments restructured the court system to more closely follow a European system of justice, and also introduced strict anticorruption rules for judges that include extensive disclosure of assets, family ties, and associations.

LAW AND ORDER

Direct enforcement of laws is handled by the *militsya* (mih-LIH-tsiah), the Ukrainian police, under the auspices of the Ministry of Home Affairs. Militiamen wearing dark blue uniforms and armed with handguns and clubs walk through the streets of Ukrainian cities or cruise in highway patrol cars. Recently, special militia forces armed with automatic weapons have also appeared.

Decades of confrontation between the people and the government in the totalitarian past have created a very suspicious attitude toward law-enforcement bodies. Ukrainians tend to not trust authorities in general, and remain convinced that involving the police brings more trouble than good. As a result, many people try to resolve conflicts among themselves, calling for the police only when there is no other option.

THE MILITARY

A mandatory two-year military service is required of all men in good health, starting at the age of eighteen. There are some exemptions from military service: those who are an only child supporting elderly parents, those with serious health problems, or those with a family of their own and at least two children born before the father's draft age. College students are sometimes exempted, depending on the political climate in the Verkhovna Rada. Wealthy families or friends of those in positions of authority often "buy" exemptions for their sons. Professional military men and women join the armed forces after graduating from military academies. Volunteers can apply without special military education. Military service for women is voluntary.

LOCAL GOVERNMENT

The structure of the government is hierarchical, with the federal government at the top of the ladder. Below that are oblasts, or districts, each with its own oblast administration, as well as a local version of parliament called the Oblast Council of People's Deputies. Elections to the Oblast Council are held every

The coat of arms (Tryzub) features a blue shield with a yellow trident. The history of the trident symbol is more than one thousand years old. The first known archaeological and historical evidence of it has been found on the seals of the Rurik dynasty. The oldest seal is that of Prince Sviatoslav Ihorevych. Although there is no sure and definite interpretation of the symbol, most historians agree that it probably depicts a stylized hawk or other totem of the first Rurik rulers' family.

four years, with each of the elected deputies representing a division within their oblast. The oblast administration is responsible for local governmental affairs, but since its powers are limited, it often only enforces the decisions of the federal government. The head of the oblast administration is the chairman of the Oblast Executive Committee, a position that changes quite often.

Rayon (county) government is a smaller model of the oblast government; it exercises even less autonomy. A city council represents the interests of residents in cities and towns. The chairperson of the city council, comparable to a mayor, is elected by the population of the city at large. It is the chairperson's duty to assemble an executive committee, members of which are approved or rejected by the city council.

INTERNET LINKS

http://www.bbc.com/news/world-europe-18006247
BBC News presents an up-to-date profile of Ukraine's president.

http://www.kmu.gov.ua/control/en
The official portal of the Ukrainian government provides news and information in English.

ECONOMY

The port of Odessa on the Black Sea is a major seaport and transportation hub.

4

STRUGGLING TO BECOME A successful independent nation is hard enough for any country, especially after having spent the better part of the last century as a reluctant part of the Soviet behemoth. The newly-independent Ukraine's economic situation presented a myriad of deep-rooted problems that have taken decades to try to overcome, and that job is far from complete. Now, however, Ukraine finds itself at war with its neighbor and former top trading partner, Russia—and this only hurts and hinders its economic progress all the more.

Ukraine is one of the richest nations in the world in terms of natural resources. Before independence, Ukraine produced 25 percent of the Soviet Union's industrial output, 25 percent of its agricultural output, 30 percent of its meat, and 50 percent of its iron ore.

An overwhelming majority of Ukraine's people voted for independence not only because they wanted the freedom of cultural expression, but also because they wanted to be masters of their land and resources. Expectations of immediate prosperity, however, soon dissipated. The gross domestic product (GDP) dropped 52 percent,

The world's deepest subway station is located in Kiev. The Arsenalna metro station is 344 feet (105 m) underground. The station, built in 1960, is deeper than the height of the Statue of Liberty. Two consecutive escalators take people down to the subway platform, and back up again. Subway passengers disembarking at this station must fervently hope the up escalators are working!

industrial output shrank 48 percent, and farm production fell 51 percent. Unemployment went up.

CHANGE AND CHALLENGES

Ukrainians were forced to acknowledge the sobering reality of their economic situation. Transitioning from a centrally-controlled communist economy to a market economy was a tough task. The economy had been badly mismanaged by the Soviet government. Inefficient and nonproductive industries—many of which are located in Ukraine's eastern regions—had been subsidized and propped up by the Soviet state. Once that support disappeared, the system's inherent failures became apparent.

Problems in energy transmissions, poor and inefficient public services, a lack of transparency and "rule of law" in the judicial and law-enforcement systems, and general poverty were urgent problems. Widespread corruption often crushed reform efforts.

Frustration with the slow pace of change prompted many Ukrainian professionals to seek employment abroad. This costly brain and talent drain further hindered economic development.

In 2000, Ukraine's economy began to turn around. Large-scale privatization picked up steam despite obstruction from certain ruling elites. Ukrainians elected a reform-minded president, but the political infighting and chaos, coupled with the global economic meltdown of 2008, sent the economy into a tailspin.

CRISIS IN THE EAST

In 2014, political turmoil in Ukraine came to a head. That year, Ukraine's economy shrunk by 6.8 percent, and in 2015, it contracted by another 9.9 percent. The purchasing power of the average person fell even more. In 2013 eight hryvnias, the Ukrainian banknote, bought one American dollar; in 2017, it took more than twenty-five hryvnias.

Prior to Russia's annexation of Crimea and the outbreak of war in the eastern border regions, Russia had been Ukraine's top trade partner. As the crisis in the East wore on, Western-leaning Ukraine looked to the European Union to help open up new markets. In 2016, the Deep and Comprehensive Free Trade Agreement (DCFTA) between Ukraine and the European Union came into force, which was aimed at helping the Ukraine's economy to recover.

In March 2017, Ukrainian President Petro Poroshenko halted all trade with the two Russian-controlled separatist regions, adding an economic angle to the military engagement there. Rail shipments, mostly of coal, out of the regions were blocked, and nothing but humanitarian aid was to be allowed in.

INDUSTRY

Ukraine has a large supply of natural resources, including around 5 percent of the world's mineral deposits. The country is especially rich in iron ore, coal, manganese, uranium ore, natural gas, oil, salt, sulfur, graphite, titanium, magnesium, kaolin, nickel, and mercury. The chemical industry produces mineral fertilizers, sulfuric acid, coke products, synthetic fibers, caustic soda, and petrochemicals.

The world's largest excavator digs for minerals at a mine in Ukraine.

Most of Ukraine's heavy industry is located in the Donetsk Basin area of Luhansk and Donetsk, also called the Donbas. This is the same eastern region of the country in which the government has been fighting pro-Russian separatist groups since 2014. Industrial production there, which was already weak, has plummeted or stopped altogether since the crisis began. Airports, mines, and factories have been destroyed or closed.

There has been some good news. In 2016, industrial growth in other sectors—such as pharmaceuticals, motor vehicles, and computers and electronics, among others—in geographic locations away from the war zone showed some improvement.

A Ukrainian miner at the Chelyuskintsev mine in Donetsk performs hard labor in low light and dirty conditions.

ENERGY

Ukraine has huge energy needs and depends on imports to meet about three-fourths of its annual oil and natural gas requirements, and 100 percent of its nuclear fuel needs. The country had been especially dependent on Russia for energy resources. Disagreements between Ukraine and Russia over natural gas prices predate the Crimea and Donbas crisis, but since 2014, the situation has become quite dire. In 2015, in light of the disintegration of relations between the countries, Ukraine announced it was weaning itself of Russian natural gas. Unfortunately, it found it couldn't provide enough gas on its own during the particularly cold winter season that followed, which only exacerbated the country's crisis situation. A trade war has cut off business between the hostile neighbors.

Coal is Ukraine's main fossil fuel. Much of the country's mining industry is concentrated in the Donbas, where there are rich deposits of coal and iron ore. Even before the outbreak of hostilities in the region, the industry was doing poorly. As in many countries, the coal industry had been in decline for decades. Low productivity, difficult and dangerous working conditions, and the switch to environmentally cleaner fuels have long affected the industry. The military actions in coal country only increased Ukraine's acute energy shortages.

Ukraine also relies on thermal, hydroelectric, and nuclear power plants for electricity. It has ten hydroelectric plants and about fifteen thermal power plants which use coal and natural gas. Ukraine also has four operating nuclear plants, with the Zaporizhia Nuclear Power Station being the largest in Europe and the third largest in the world. However, the plant's location near the city of Enerhodar is a matter of concern, as it is 124 miles (200 km) from the combat zone in the Donbas.

A hydroelectric dam on the Dnieper River in Nova Kakhovka in southern Ukraine.

TRANSPORTATION

The railway system in Ukraine has been developed extensively and is the twelfth largest in the world. There is hardly a town in Ukraine with a population over ten thousand that does not have a railway station, both for freight and passenger trains. Railways dominate the transportation network of the country.

Waterways are also used extensively for transportation needs. Major rivers, such as the Dnieper, the Dnister, and the Pivdenny Bug, as well as the Azov and Black Seas, provide transportation routes for ships and barges year-round. The Black Sea Shipping Company (BLASCO) is one of the largest transportation enterprises in the world.

Ukraine's aviation sector is developing quickly, having established a visa-free program for EU nationals and citizens of a number of other Western nations. However, the war in the Donbas has hindered this growth, as it

UKRAINIAN CURRENCY

A temporary "transition period" currency was introduced in 1992, replacing the Russian ruble, the currency used all across the former Soviet Union. The Ukrainian word for the temporary currency was karbovanets (kahr-BOH-vah-nets), though it was often called "coupon." When the coupons were first introduced, there were 1, 3, 5, 10, 25, 50, and 100 karbovanet notes. Later on, because of hyperinflation, these notes became collectors' items. By the first quarter of 1996, the smallest bill

was 1,000 and the largest 10,000,000. The rate of exchange in 1996 was approximately 150,000 karbovanets to the US dollar, so even 10 million karbovanets equaled only $68.

By the third quarter of 1996, the government was finally able to introduce a new Ukrainian currency, called the hryvnia *(HRIV-nah), named after a currency used in ancient Kievan Rus. Its currency sign is* ₴. *Today the hryvnia (above) is in circulation as a stable medium of exchange in the country and is maintaining a healthy rate of exchange. Some people, however, prefer the US dollar or the euro for currency whenever possible.*

has affected much of the economy. Donetsk Sergey Prokofiev International Airport, for example, was destroyed after a series of battles took place there in 2014 and 2015. Similarly, Luhansk International Airport was mostly destroyed and closed in 2014.

The country's airline, Ukraine International Airlines, is based in Kiev with its main hub at Boryspil International Airport, which handles most of Ukraine's international air traffic. In 2015, following the Russian annexation of Crimea and the continued fighting in the Donbas region, Ukraine banned flights from Russia from landing in the country, and Russia responded in kind. In 2017, Ukraine hoped to see the completion of a new terminal at Odessa International Airport, which was begun in 2012.

In large cities there are buses and subways. Public transportation is inexpensive and relatively efficient, but during rush hour, passengers can be packed tightly—a familiar experience in New York and other major cities, too. In remote areas of the country, however, trains may be slower and break down rather frequently.

AGRICULTURE

Agricultural land accounts for nearly 70 percent of the total land area in Ukraine, but agriculture itself accounts for only 14.4 percent of its gross domestic product. A mere 5.8 percent of the country's labor force works in this industry.

Agricultural success in Ukraine is attributed to its industrious farmers, a moderate climate, and some of the most fertile black soil in the world—chernozem ("black earth"). The production of grains and oilseeds is always the main topic with Ukrainian producers and policy makers. The country is

Seasonal workers harvest onions.

Although travel sites continue to tout the wonders of Ukraine, the war in the Donblass has naturally had a dampening effect on the country's tourism sector. The number of foreign visitors fell from about 24.7 million in 2013 to 12.7 million in 2014. Most tourists come from Eastern Europe, with by far the largest number, 4.3 million in 2016, coming from Moldova, Ukraine's small neighbor to its west. The number of Russian tourists, in particular, fell by 77 percent in one year.

The war, however, is largely confined to the east, and the capital Kiev—the country's major tourism destination—remains reasonably safe. Among the city's attractions are the beautiful golden-domed cathedrals, especially the Kyevo-Pecherska Lavra monastery complex. The Taras Shevchenko National Opera Theater is a center for classical music and ballet, and there are a number of museums, including the Pyrohovo Museum of Folk Architecture, one of Europe's largest open-air museums.

Ukraine boasts seven UNESCO World Heritage sites, including Saint Sophia Cathedral and the monastery

The National Opera Theater in Kiev is a center of culture.

complex mentioned here, as well as the historic center of L'viv. For tourism purposes, Ukraine also came up with the "Seven Wonders of Ukraine," a listing of the country's top architectural and natural attractions, which were determined by popular vote in 2007. Unfortunately, one of those Seven Wonders—the remains of the ancient Greek city of Chersonesus, which is also UNESCO World Heritage site, is located in Sevastopol, Crimea. Given the Russian annexation of Crimea in 2014, it currently lies beyond the reach of Ukraine.

the world's fifth-biggest seller of wheat and other grains. Wheat, barley, rapeseed (a source of vegetable oil), and sunflowers make up about 55 percent of the country's total agricultural output. Corn, sugar beets, and soybeans are also major crops. Except for the farms and processing plants located in the Donbas region, the conflict in Ukraine's East hasn't had much of a negative effect on the industry in the rest of the country.

Ukraine's famously rich soil makes it a natural for the organic food market. Hundreds of thousands of Ukrainian acres are already devoted to organic farming, and this sector could easily expand to meet the increasing demand in Western Europe for such products.

On the other hand, the dairy industry suffered from the crisis because Russia had previously accounted for 80 percent of dairy exports. On January 1, 2016, Russia completely banned imported food products from Ukraine. That same month, the European Commission granted Ukrainian milk processing companies access to the EU market. The first country to receive Ukrainian dairy products was Bulgaria.

Dairy cows produce milk for exports.

INTERNET LINKS

http://emerging-europe.com/category/special-reports/ukraine-2017
This site offers a variety of up-to-date stories relating to Ukraine's economy.

http://www.ukraine-arabia.ae/economy
This site offers a comprehensive overview of Ukraine's economy, with updates regarding the effects of the war in the Donbas.

ENVIRONMENT

Factory chimneys spew smoke into the air in Kiev's industrial zone.

5

U KRAINE INHERITED AN ABUNDANCE of environmental problems from its years as republic of the Soviet Union. The greatest of these was surely the nuclear meltdown at Chernobyl in 1986, one of the greatest environmental disasters of the twentieth century. Its effects linger on in all the living things in the region, as well as in the contaminated soil and water. Parts of the radiation polluted land will never again be fit for human habitation.

The legacy of Soviet-era damage to the environment reaches well beyond Chernobyl. In the final two decades of Soviet rule, the industrialization of Ukraine, especially in the Donetsk basin, created serious air pollution, contaminated the Dnieper River, and contributed to the deterioration of the Black Sea.

Corruption, an ongoing problem for many sectors in Ukraine, has undermined numerous attempts at cleaning up the environment.

WASTE

Waste management in Ukraine is far below modern norms, with all sorts of waste products—medical, electronic, construction, household, and

In the restricted area surrounding the Chernobyl nuclear accident site, wildlife is popularly said to be flourishing, mainly due to the lack of human activity. However, scientific studies have found evidence of increased genetic deformities, tumors, and other effects of radiation. Birds' brains were found to be 5 percent smaller, and in some places, 40 percent of male birds are sterile. Biodiversity is down by about 50 percent.

even toxic—accumulating in unregulated landfills. Recycling is far below the levels of most Western European countries. Toxic and hazardous wastes are stockpiled across the country. Toxic industrial wastes from defunct industrial plants are haphazardly stored at numerous locations without sufficient environmental protection or oversight. The waste contaminates the local groundwater supplies and, with each storm or flood event, routinely overflows into nearby streams. In turn, this pollutes drinking water supplies, severely contaminates aquatic ecosystems.

Overfilled trash containers spill garbage onto the street in Lviv.

AIR POLLUTION

Since independence, Ukraine has encouraged the formation of numerous environmental organizations, and as a result, there is general awareness among the people of the harmful effects of air pollution. Grave environmental damages of the Soviet past have come to light and have been replaced by more environmentally friendly legislation, regulation, and practice.

As in most other countries, however, a major source of pollution in large cities is road traffic. The chemical industry also adds to air pollution, and oil refineries pollute underground waters. No substantial progress has been achieved in pollution control by the machine-making industry. Although its share in the total emissions of pollutants is relatively small, the specific contaminants present are much more hazardous to health than in other industries.

WILDLIFE

More than forty thousand species of animals live in Ukraine, including the water areas of the Black Sea and the Sea of Azov. The country has thirty-three wetland conservation sites, three biosphere nature reserves, and three national parks. A wide variety of birds are found in the country, including

THE BLACK SEA AND THE SEA OF AZOV

The coasts of the Black Sea and the adjoining Sea of Azov make up much of the southern borders of Ukraine (including Russian-occupied Crimea and the separatist-occupied oblast of Donetsk). They stretch over five administrative units, or oblasts, and the total length of the coastline is more than 1,865 miles (3,000 km).

The Black Sea and the Sea of Azov are home to nearly 160 species of fish. The Black Sea has fish of Mediterranean origin that make up about 60 percent of the marine population there.

Exhaustive economic development over the last decades has resulted in considerable ecological pressure and imbalance to the area. This has led to great changes in the natural conditions of the seas, causing pollution.

One of the negative effects is seashore erosion caused by dredging and hydromechanical works conducted in the territorial waters and on the Black Sea shelf. Around 245 acres (100 ha) of land is washed away annually. This causes territories to shrink, hindering town planning and tourism development, and negatively affecting the coastline's ecological system. The few measures to protect the seashore are fragmented and do not constitute a joint protection system along the entire Ukrainian coastline. Following the adoption of several governmental regulations, about 95 miles (150 km) of the shore has been reinforced.

about one hundred species of migratory birds. Some of the endangered bird species include the black stork, black and Griffon vultures, osprey, and golden eagle. The wetlands of southern Ukraine, such as Syvash, are places of particular importance as they are home to hundreds of thousands of birds.

On April 26, 1986, when Ukraine was still a part of the Soviet Union, the fourth reactor at the Chernobyl nuclear power plant exploded. The Chernobyl nuclear power plant is near the town of Pripyat, north of Kiev near the Belarus border. The accident and fire that followed released an enormous amount of radioactive material into the environment, contaminating huge territories surrounding the site.

The explosion released about 9 tons of nuclear-reactive materials into the air—about four hundred times more radiation than the atomic bombing of Hiroshima, Japan, during World War II. The town of Pripyat wasn't evacuated until thirty-six hours after the incident. Much of the contamination was deposited close to Chernobyl, in parts of Belarus, Ukraine, and Russia. After the incident, however, traces of radioactive deposits were found in nearly every country in the northern hemisphere. Wind currents and uneven rainfall left some areas more heavily contaminated than their immediate neighbors. The Chernobyl disaster is one of only two nuclear accidents classified as a level 7 event (the maximum classification) on the International Nuclear Event Scale. The other is Japan's Fukushima Daiichi nuclear disaster in 2011.

The Soviet Union did not immediately release news of the nuclear accident. (This was not unusual; the USSR often tried to keep internal problems a secret from the outside world.) In fact, the world didn't know until two days later, when workers at a nuclear power plant in Sweden—some 680 miles (1,100 km) away—were found to have radioactive particles in their clothing, and upon investigating, the source of the radioactivity was ultimately discovered.

The number of deaths caused by the Chernobyl accident remains highly controversial. Thirty-one people died at or shortly after the time of the event, including seven firefighters. Most died of acute radiation syndrome. The deaths and illnesses caused by the long-term effects of radiation are more difficult to determine and are still being investigated. The workers involved in the recovery and cleanup after the disaster, called "liquidators"—as

many as six hundred thousand people—were insufficiently protected and received high doses of radiation. A United Nations study estimated the total number of premature deaths due to radiation exposure to be around four thousand. Humans were not the only ones affected. In the four years following the event, farmers in the region reported some 350 animals were born with gross deformities.

Once the reactor fires had been extinguished, a sarcophagus encasing was constructed by the Soviets to entomb the fourth reactor. The encasing was built in haste, however, and began crumbling. Despite reinforcing, there were fears it would collapse and release tons more of radioactive dust. A replacement shelter, the New Safe Confinement (below), designed to last one hundred years, was started in 2007 and was expected to be completed by the end of 2017. The new shelter will contain the radioactive materials and prevent further environmental contamination.

Authorities eventually evacuated 91,200 people from the nuclear plant's surrounding area and restricted it as the Chernobyl Exclusion Zone. Its boundaries were later expanded. Today it is the one of the most contaminated places on earth. The city of Pripyat is a ghost town. Nevertheless, a few hundred people either refused to evacuate or sneaked back in and resumed living there. In 2017, there were fewer than two hundred mostly elderly such people living in eleven villages inside the Exclusion Zone. The power plant itself, aside from the destroyed reactor, continued to operate until it was finally closed down in 2000.

The griffon vulture is an endangered scavenger species in Ukraine.

The Red Book of Ukraine, an official list of rare and endangered species of animals, plants, and fungi, names those species that are protected from illegal hunting, trapping, or collecting, and identifies protected natural areas of great importance for the animals.

WATER USE AND MANAGEMENT

The government of Ukraine is now focusing on increasing the accessibility to clean drinking water. The lack of this poses significant health and environmental concerns to the Ukrainian populace. Although nearly the entire population has access to safe drinking water, the current network is overexploited. As a result of the rising population pressure on the limited supply of potable water, many cities receive water only twice a day for a limited number of hours. Tourists are advised not to drink tap water, and many Ukrainians drink bottled water or water from wells in rural areas.

The country's main water basins are the Dnieper, the Dniester, the Danube, the Siversky Donetsk, and the Southern Bug. All these basins drain south toward the Black Sea and the Sea of Azov. The Dnieper, the major river, is fed by several tributaries and divides the country into two parts. Six large reservoirs built on the river provide water for the industrial centers of Donbas, for irrigation in Crimea and the Black Sea coast, and for hydropower generation. About 60 percent of the population depends on the Dnieper for its drinking-water supply.

In 1999, apart from the rivers in Crimea, all river basins in Ukraine were classified either as polluted or very polluted. Most of the pollution came from agricultural activity. Mining and industrial activities have also contributed to the pollution, although the volume of effluence has declined as a result of the industrial recession. Untreated industrial and animal wastes, indiscriminate discharges of toxic sewage, excessive fertilization, and runoff from areas hit by the Chernobyl incident are some of the pollutants that render many of Ukraine's water resources unsafe for consumption even today.

INTERNET LINKS

http://www.bbc.com/news/world-europe-36115240
This BBC presentation explores the Chernobyl nuclear disaster with many photos and links to related stories.

http://news.nationalgeographic.com/2017/01/illegal-amber-mining-ukraine
This in-depth article presents a beautifully photographed look at the environmental harm of Ukraine's amber industry.

http://www.politico.eu/interactive/in-pictures-chernobyl-30-years-later
This 2016 post is an extraordinary photo essay about Chernobyl thirty years after the disaster.

http://www.ukrweekly.com/uwwp/ukraines-afflicted-environment
Ukraine Weekly's article gives a broad overview of Ukraine's environmental problems.

UKRANIANS

A group of young people in Kiev show their pride in Ukrainian culture.

6

T HE CONSTITUTION OF UKRAINE refers to all of the country's 44.2 million citizens as Ukrainians, regardless of ethnicity. Most of them, 78 percent, are also considered ethnic Ukrainians. They are the descendants of the Slavic peoples of the ancient state of Kievan Rus. The second largest group of Ukrainian citizens, making up 17 percent of the population, is ethnically Russian. The remaining 5 percent include Byelorussians, Moldavians, Bulgarians, Crimean Tatars, Jews, and Roma.

Although the population numbers are trending downward, Ukraine is still one of the most densely populated countries in Europe.

These ethnic groups are not spread evenly throughout the country, however. By far, most Ukrainians of Russian background live in Crimea or the eastern border regions, where, in some places, they make up more than half of the population. Crimea, in particular, was more than 58 percent Russian in 2001, according to the most recent Ukrainian census. (The next census will take place in 2020.) This ethnic—and corresponding language—imbalance has created a social, demographic divide that threatens the nation's unity. The loyalty of Ukraine's ethnic Russians to Russia has encouraged Russian aggression in Crimea and the east. Russia's annexation of Crimea in 2014 and the ongoing war in the eastern regions of Luhansk and Donetsk are clearly impacting Ukraine's sovereignty.

MINORITIES

Ukraine is a fairly homogeneous society. Nonetheless, there are small groups of people living in the central and southwestern areas who differ from the mainstream Ukrainians, although they are related ethnically. Until 1946 the Lemko people lived throughout the Carpathian Mountains on both the eastern and western sides. Now they are confined to a small area in the westernmost part of Ukraine. Only recently the Lemkos exchanged their traditional dress, called a *chuhy* (CHOO-hee), a woolen covering without sleeves, for modern clothes.

The Boikos, or Highlanders, are mountaineers who live slightly farther east than the Lemkos. Their main occupation is cattle breeding. The Boikos have maintained many of their ancient customs, particularly in architecture. The area they inhabit is spotted with old-style churches and wooden houses with large entrance halls. Even today it is not uncommon to see a Boiko man or woman—dressed in a traditional long cloak decorated with beads—tilling the soil using traditional agricultural tools.

The Volhynians inhabit the northern mountain areas. They are known for their musical talents, especially lyre playing and singing. Their festive carols and religious songs have been particularly well preserved.

The most notable of the ethnic minorities are the Hutsuls, who breed cattle and sheep and are heavily engaged in forestry. They are known throughout Ukraine for their exceptional craftsmanship and building techniques. Wood carving, pottery making, brass work, and rug weaving are among the highly developed Hutsul crafts. For hundreds of years, the Hutsuls have carved objects made of wood, such as doors, chests, and crosses, with intricate geometric patterns and beaded inlays. Today their handicrafts are sold throughout Ukraine, some commanding very high prices.

THE TATARS

The Turkic peoples can be divided into two main groups, eastern and western. The eastern Turks, which include people living in Turkey and regions of the former Soviet Union, including Crimea, are sometimes characterized as dark-skinned, but many are as fair as western Europeans.

The western Turks, called Tatars, consist of two groups—those living in the former Tatar Autonomous Soviet Socialist Republic (ASSR), located in the middle of the Volga River basin, and those inhabiting the Crimean Peninsula. The peninsula was incorporated into the Crimean ASSR in 1921 and continued to be populated primarily by Tatars. In 1944, the republic was abolished and the Tatars were deported to Siberia and Central Asia for allegedly collaborating with the Nazis.

Although their homeland was officially rehabilitated in 1967, the Crimean Tatars were not permitted to return to it, and only after the dissolution of the Soviet Union did they begin to trickle back.

The Tatars are well known as traders, but they also have an ancient tradition of craftsmanship in wood, ceramics, leather, cloth, and metal. During the ninth to the fifteenth centuries, the Tatar economy became based on a combination of farming and herding that continues to this day.

In February 2017, people march in Kiev to show support for the Crimean Tatars and other Ukrainians residing in Russian-occupied Crimea.

DIASPORA

A large number of Ukrainians can also be found throughout the world. Emigrants have had several reasons for leaving home—escaping political oppression, cruel landlords, and unbearable economic hardships.

Massive emigration from Ukraine occurred at the beginning of the twentieth century when continuous turmoil in Russia caused many people to search for better living conditions abroad. After the Communists took over in Ukraine, there were a number of dissidents who preferred (or were forced) to live abroad rather than submit to Communist rule. Aside from Russia itself, the largest number of Ukrainians live in Canada, followed by the United States.

NATIONAL FEATURES

Despite invasion and occupation by foreign conquerors and the number of minorities living in the country, Ukrainians have retained their predominantly Slavic physical features. The expression *schyryy ukrayinets* (SHCHIH-riy ook-rah-YI-nets), meaning "sheer Ukrainian," is more a reflection of the dominant features of the unique Ukrainian character than of physical features.

A typical Ukrainian may have dark or blond hair, and gray, blue, or brown eyes, and as a people their personalities may be just as diverse. But one thing that all Ukrainians are taught from the time they are young is hospitality.

When there is a guest in the house, whether staying for several hours or several days, the host's personal life is sacrificed almost completely. In extreme cases, many Ukrainians will take leave from their jobs and provide the guest with the best possible accommodation, even if it means temporarily giving up their bedrooms.

Feeding a guest is also part of Ukrainian hospitality, and no expense is spared to ensure that the meal is well prepared and the guest well fed. Children are taught at a young age that providing a good meal for a guest is the most important obligation in hospitality. As a result, many visitors have left Ukraine with the mistaken impression that Ukrainians eat like royalty every night of the week.

NATIONAL DRESS

Traditional national dress for both women and men is characterized by intricate embroidery with distinct variations in style, depending on the

district of Ukraine it comes from. Nowadays, the Ukrainian national dress is worn only at folk festivals.

Men's dress is simpler than that of women, consisting of very loose trousers, pulled tight at the waist by a sash and at the ankles by laces, and a linen shirt with long sleeves. Depending on the season, men may also wear an overcoat with long, wide sleeves, and a hat that looks something like a stocking cap. Boots are made of leather and worn to the knee. All the garments are worn loose to allow for ease in movement. This is because Ukrainian national dress dates back to the time of the Cossacks when clothing had to be loose and suitable for fighting.

In earlier times, it was easy to distinguish between a married and an unmarried woman, since Orthodox Church rules obliged a married woman to cover her hair with a kerchief. Unmarried women, on the other hand, wore colorful ribbons in their hair as decorations. Coral beads were worn around the neck as part of the outfit, and since a string of such beads was sometimes equal to the value of a cow, the number of strands a woman wore was an indicator of her family's wealth.

Young women wear the Ukrainian national costume at an airport welcoming ceremony.

TARAS HRYHOROVYCH SHEVCHENKO

Two books are in nearly every household in Ukraine: the Bible and Kobzar *("The Bard") by Taras Shevchenko (1814–1861). Shevchenko was born into a family of peasants in central Ukraine. From his early childhood he showed signs of genius. His love for his people and his enormous talent—he was a poet, a painter, and an engraver—changed the son of illiterate serfs into the enlightened prophet of the Ukrainian people, a creator of the Ukrainian literary language, and an inspiration for generations of Ukrainian independence fighters. Monuments to Shevchenko stand in nearly every town and in any place in the world where there is a significant population of Ukrainians. There is a monument in Washington, DC, erected by Ukrainian Americans acknowledging the poet's achievements.*

When performing Ukrainian folk dances, women now wear a unique style of dress traditional to their part of the country. A brightly colored woolen skirt is worn over a petticoat and covered with a white apron. An embroidered white blouse called a *vyshyvanka* is typical, and sometimes worn with a vest. On their heads, women wear a floral headdress with streamers flowing down the back.

In western Ukraine, there are some significant differences in national dress. This is explained by the influence of neighboring Hungary, Poland, and Romania. At folk festivals, men wear tight pants, sometimes vests, and tight overcoats. Their hats are round, with moderately wide rims, and decorated with rooster's feathers. The women have distinctive headpieces and wear skirts tied at the waist and sometimes open at the front to reveal another embroidered layer.

UKRAINIAN NAMES

Ukrainian names are partially of Slavic origin, partially of biblical origin, sometimes borrowed from Greece (because of the Byzantine influence), and, recently, adopted from other European nations.

Names of Slavic origin date to pagan times and usually reflect the qualities for which men and women were admired in those days. For example, Svitlana, meaning "full of light"; Liudmyla, "loved by people"; Volodymyr, "world owner"; and Myroslav, "praised by the community," are all popular Slavic names.

Sometimes Ukrainian spelling and pronunciation disguises the relation of Ukrainian names to the equivalent names in English. For example, John in English is Ivan in Ukrainian, and Mary is Mariya.

Ukrainian last names are derived from male ancestors' names. Ivanchuk, for example, most likely had a distant male ancestor named Ivan. Other names, such as Kovalchuk, an exact equivalent of the name Smith, were derived from professional skills.

Ukrainians do not have middle names. Instead, they use patronymic names, which are formed by adding a suffix to the name of the person's father. For example, the patronymic of a woman whose father's name is Ivan, is Ivanivna, and her brother's patronymic is Ivanovych. When meeting someone for the first time in Ukraine, it is polite to call them by their first and patronymic names, rather than using only the first name or last name. For example, "I'm happy to meet you, Mariya Ivanivna."

INTERNET LINKS

http://www.bbc.com/news/world-europe-26387353
This BBC article examines the problem of ethnic divisions in Ukraine.

http://www.encyclopediaofukraine.com/People.asp
This site provides a good historical overview of the Ukrainian people.

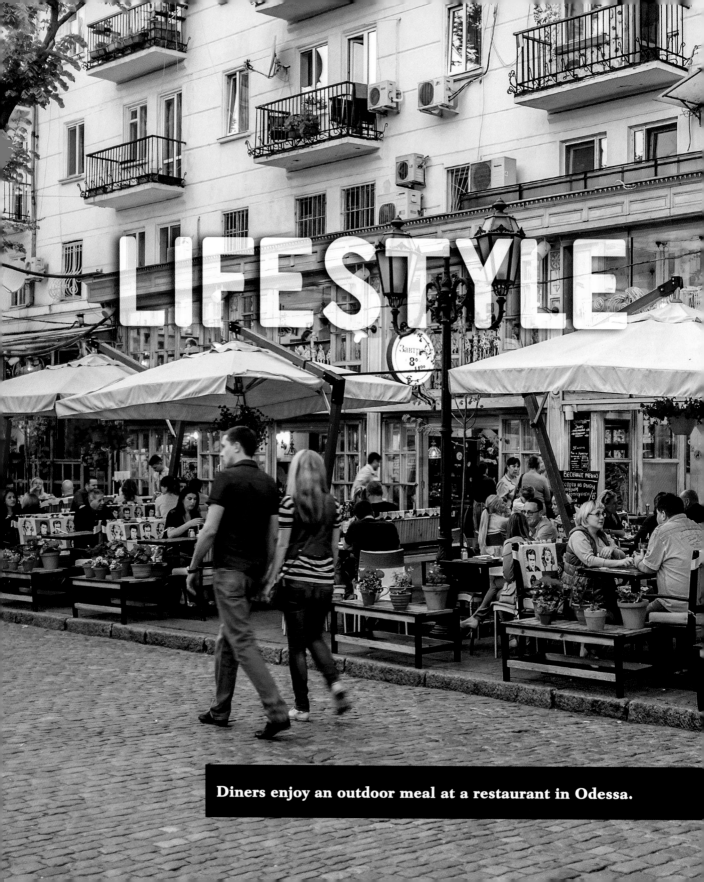

LIFESTYLE

Diners enjoy an outdoor meal at a restaurant in Odessa.

7

UKRAINE HAS AN ANCIENT agricultural heritage, but the majority of its population is urban. In recent years, migration to urban centers has caused tremendous population growth in the cities. This urban movement is usually perpetuated by the desire for a higher standard of living. In the city, one can enjoy concerts, movies, shopping centers, restaurants, a developed system of public transportation, central heating, direct long-distance telephone dialing, and cable television. In the country, there are no concert halls, few movie theaters, no public transportation, no cable television (and television in general is limited to one or two channels), no central heating (which means in many cases using coal and wood stoves all winter long), and no telephones, or, for the few people who have them, limited options for long-distance calling.

In the country, the roads are dry and dusty in the summer, wet and muddy in the autumn and spring, and deep in snow and ice in the winter. Shopping is confined to one or two small "products" stores (the equivalent of grocery stores). Since few people own cars, trips to a city are rare and tiring. Bus schedules are unreliable and fares are costly.

The cities provide a wide range of educational options. There are no colleges in rural areas, which means in order to pursue a career other than farming or mining, Ukrainians must travel to the city to study. Taking everything into consideration, many people sacrifice the advantages of rural life—fresh air, natural food, low crime rates, and a quiet pace of life—for a more hectic but more convenient lifestyle in the cities.

HOUSING

Ukrainians live in private houses on farms and in small towns. Although this may seem like a luxury to some, Ukrainians who live in houses do not necessarily do so by choice. There are few apartment buildings other than

Deribasivska Street is the main thoroughfare in downtown Odessa, the port city on the Black Sea. It's a lively tourist attraction, but it also has an unusual history. After the Russian Revolution of 1917, street names were changed to honor Soviet functionaries. In 1920 Deribasivska Street, named to commemorate one of Odessa's honorary citizens, General José De Ribas, was renamed Lassalya Street, in honor of one of the Russian revolutionaries. Plates with the new name replaced old ones on the walls of the houses along the street. But by morning the plates had disappeared, and chalk and paint had been used to inscribe the old name. Numerous attempts to mount the new plates on the street failed, and finally the Soviet authorities gave up. Thus Deribasivska Street kept its name throughout the decades, much to the pride of the city's residents.

those in large cities. With the recent growth in urban areas, inadequate housing has become a problem. Because the socialist order claimed to provide free services to its citizens, theoretically housing was free for everyone. Registering with a city administration was all any citizen needed to do to be assigned a place to live.

The standards were very low and many families shared one kitchen, but some apartments had the advantage of a few modern conveniences, such as indoor bathrooms and central heating. Apartments like these were owned by the city, so the rent was insignificant and the utilities were very cheap. The catch was to acquire the apartment as soon as possible after someone vacated, because in some cases the waiting list consisted of a thousand names. In these cases a family had to live with parents or rent an apartment from private owners, which could cost up to 25 percent of their monthly income for ten years or more, while waiting.

Private ownership was discouraged since construction and repair materials were either in short supply or unbearably expensive, and services were difficult to obtain. Even if building a house were an option, people preferred to live in an apartment where they were responsible only for maintaining the interior.

After independence, occupants had the option to buy or sell apartments in which they had been living. Many families could not afford the upkeep of larger apartments because utilities became very expensive, so they had to sell their apartments and buy smaller ones. For some, the living conditions were worse but just the knowledge of owning their own home was enough.

BACKYARD FARMING

Under the Communist regime, wages earned from working on a collective farm very rarely met the needs of the average Ukrainian family. While members of a collective farm enjoyed discount prices for products produced on-site, there was rarely enough cash to spare for anything but other kinds of food. The solution for many families was to plant vegetables in a small plot of land near their house, a kind of extended backyard with a few fruit trees, a cow or two in a small barn, several chickens, and three or four pigs. This type of private farming helped collective farmers to extend their food choices and to support their families, because any surplus could be sold at the farmers' market in the nearest town.

Even those living in small towns in private houses began using their backyards for raising fresh vegetables, eggs, and meat for their tables—and sometimes a little cash.

UKRAINIAN WOMEN

Gender-based discrimination is against the law, but women in Ukraine tend to have lower salaries and fewer opportunities than men. On average, women earn about 30 percent less than men who do similar work. Attitudes of men have been slow to change. A woman in Ukraine would be lucky indeed if her husband helped her in the kitchen, to say nothing of his ever taking complete

If Ukrainian women are supposed to be satisfied with traditional female roles, Yulia Tymoshenko (b. 1960) never got the memo. Born in the city of Dnipropetrovsk during the

Soviet era, she is a Ukrainian politician who served as the first woman prime minister of Ukraine for several months in 2005 and again from 2007 to 2010. She was a leader of the Orange Revolution in 2004 and became a very vocal critic of several of Ukraine's top leaders and their administrations. She has run for president several times. When she ran for president in 2010, candidate Viktor Yanukovych refused to debate her, saying that "a woman's place is in the kitchen."

It's also worth noting that after Yanukovich won the election, Tymoshenko was accused and convicted of embezzlement and abuse of power. (It was not the first time she had faced corruption charges.) She was sentenced to seven years in prison and ordered to pay the government $188 million. Many international observers, including the European Union and the United States, as well as human rights organizations, condemned the proceedings as politically motivated and called for her release.

In February 2014, after President Yanukovich fled the country in the wake of the Euromaidan protests, Tymoshenko was released. She continues to be very involved in Ukraine's politics. She favors having Ukraine join the EU and NATO, and remains wary of Russia. She is said to be Ukraine's most famous and most controversial public figure.

charge of cleaning the house and running other errands, like shopping for food—an exhausting daily obligation. Instead, the principle that "he brings home the money, she runs the home" is widely practiced. The irony of this is that Ukraine's economy makes it impossible for a man to earn enough to support his entire family, which means that wives must bear a double load.

Women in executive business positions are rare, and the percentage of women in parliament is small. In 2014, about 12.1 percent of the Verkhovna

Rada was female. The situation tends to be slightly better at the oblast and city levels of administration. Traditional nurturing occupations are still the most common professions for women: preschool teachers, nurses, and cooks.

Although Ukraine remains in many aspects a traditional society, in recent years several laws have been enacted by the Ukrainian government to broaden women's rights. Working women, for example, receive 126 days of maternity leave at full pay. After the leave, the woman may return to her position in the company for which she had worked. A mother can also receive sick leave from work to stay home with an ill child. By law, a father can do this as well.

FAMILY LIFE

In the last thirty years, the average family size in Ukraine has declined from five members to three. This is because many couples postpone having children until they own a place of their own. Since housing costs are exorbitant, most young couples continue to live with their parents for some years.

Despite this decline, the birth of a child is a most joyous occasion. If finances allow, Ukrainians prefer that the new mother stay at home for as long as possible. In many cases, though, a mother must return to work, particularly if a long break jeopardizes her career. In these cases the family must search elsewhere for child care. Since it is still common for three generations to live under the same roof, the responsibility of looking after the children often falls on the grandparents. If the grandparents do not live with their children, parents can turn to the well-developed network of child-care centers.

In Ukraine babies can be accepted at child-care centers when they are only eleven months old, but most parents, unless it is absolutely necessary, prefer to delay using these centers until the child has reached two or three years of age.

Unlike in many other countries, Ukrainian adult children are legally obliged to support their elderly or disabled parents. Of course, it is a moral obligation that children are taught when they are young and that they see everywhere,

so legal action is rare. Retirement facilities in Ukraine are exclusively state-run, and for the most part, conditions in such facilities are bleak.

Primary school children study at their desks in Odessa.

EDUCATION

Twelve years of schooling are mandatory in Ukraine. Schools are state-run, and any deviation from the standard curriculum, established by the Ministry of Education, is discouraged. The objective of general schooling is to give younger students a good knowledge of the fundamentals of the arts and sciences and to teach them how to use this knowledge practically.

Children start first grade at the age of six. Primary education takes four years to complete, middle school takes five, and then there are three years of high school to undergo. Ukraine's Law on Education states that provision of elementary schools must be made wherever there are students. Grades 10 to 12 are secondary school levels. After the ninth grade, Ukrainian students used to have the option of going to a vocational or technical school rather than completing their secondary school education. Vocational and technical school programs could last anywhere from one year (if entered after graduation from secondary school) to three years (if entered after the ninth grade). Today, however, secondary education is compulsory.

While in the twelfth grade, students sit for the school-leaving examinations or the Government Tests, which also serve as tests for university admission. Getting into a college or university is very competitive. Applicants are required to produce a secondary school certificate and to pass four entrance examinations. The academic year begins in September and ends in July and consists of two academic semesters. There are more than three hundred universities and academies in Ukraine, and some two hundred are state-run.

HEALTH CARE

Although the Ukrainian constitution stipulates that providing health care is one of the key functions of the state, the result has been mixed and problematic. The country's health care system was based on an obsolete Soviet model burdened with bureaucracy and inefficiency. Medical professionals were paid such low salaries that many doctors demanded supplementary payment— essentially bribes—for their services.

In 2016, Ukraine passed a landmark health care reform bill aimed at radically overhauling the country's medical services, which had been rife with corrupt business practices. The Health Ministry's three-year plan intends to remake Ukraine's healthcare system in the style of modern European practices. It plans to transfer most patient care from hospital treatment to primary care and prevention, increase funding efficiency, encourage better practices among doctors and hospitals, and ensure citizens have access to a healthcare services free of charge.

Although many hailed the initiative as a positive step, those who profited from the old, entrenched ways—pharmaceutical companies, for example— fought hard against it. Time will tell if the reformers can shake off the power elites in this sector.

SOCIAL SERVICES

The official retirement age in Ukraine is fifty-five for women and sixty for men, but is gradually being raised to sixty for women and sixty-two for men by 2021. Pensions are based on years of employment and salary averages during the final two years of service. The amount of the pension is rarely more than 50 percent of the salary.

Since independence, inflation, unstable prices, and general shortages have caused most retired people to seek part-time jobs in order to survive. There are no private retirement homes, not only because the concept itself is culturally unusual and very new, but also because the overwhelming majority of retirees would not be able to afford the charges. State-run facilities are free, but they are used only as a last resort, since the conditions there are usually quite poor.

In addition to retirement homes, there are state-run orphanages and homes for the disabled, kept running mostly by the devotion of the staff and, more recently, by donations from newly created private businesses.

INTERNET LINKS

http://www.bbc.com/news/world-europe-15249184
The BBC profile of Yulia Tymoshenko gives a good overview up to 2014.

http://euromaidanpress.com/2017/01/21/healthcare-reform-in-ukraine-under-concerted-attack-suprun
This article takes a frank look at the attempt to reform healthcare in Ukraine.

http://news.nationalpost.com/full-comment/diane-francis-ukraines-survivor-yulia-tymoshenko
This article provides an excellent portrait of Yulia Tymoshenko.

RELIGION

An Orthodox parishioner lights a candle at Easter time.

8

UKRAINE IS OVERWHELMINGLY Christian, with some 38 million people belonging to some form of Christian denomination. Eastern Orthodox Christianity is by far the dominant religion, with about 35 million followers in Ukraine. When Ukraine fell to the Russians in the seventeenth century, the Ukrainian Orthodox Church was absorbed into the Russian Orthodox Church.

Since Ukrainian independence, the country's Orthodox Church has broken into three sectors:

- the Ukrainian Orthodox Church governed by the Moscow Patriarchate (UOC—MP), which is essentially the Russian Orthodox Church (ROC);
- the Ukrainian Orthodox Church of the Kiev Patriarchate (UOC—KP), headed by Patriarch Filaret (b. 1930);
- and the Ukrainian Autocephalous (Independent) Church (UAOC).

The Moscow-headed branch is the established, officially recognized Orthodox Church in Ukraine. The other two formed—or was revived, in the case of the UAOC, which originally formed in 1921—around 1991 in order to be free of Russian influence. However, they both remain unrecognized by the ecclesiastical authorities of the Eastern Orthodox Churches, some people suspect because of pressure from the Moscow authorities.

Russian military intervention in Ukrainian territory has increased political friction in the churches. The religious authorities in some parishes tend to take sides in the conflict. Some priests of the Ukrainian Orthodox Church of the Moscow Patriarchate (Russian Orthodox) are said to be pro-Russian and have been criticized as "anti-Ukrainian." The war with Russia has driven some Ukrainians to switch to the pro-Ukrainian branches of the Church.

Today, it's hard to know exactly how many of Ukraine's population profess allegiance to which branch, but together they make up about 65 percent of the country's total population. The Autocephalus Church has about one thousand parishes, nearly seven hundred churches, and operates almost exclusively in the western areas of Ukraine. The Kievan Patriarchate is headed by and is largely found in the western provinces and the Kiev region.

Other than slight differences in the procedures of the service, the three churches are nearly identical. One difference is seen in the liturgical language used for services, which in the Western branches is closer to everyday Ukrainian.

The Ukrainian Greek Catholic Church (sometimes called the Uniate Church) has the second largest following in Ukraine. This denomination originated in 1596 for the benefit of Roman Catholic Poland, which dominated significant parts of Ukraine at the time. The Ukrainian Greek Catholic Church follows the Eastern rite, while recognizing the leadership of the pope in Rome. There are between three million and five million faithful Greek Catholics, most of whom live in the western part of Ukraine, which was ruled by the Poles for centuries.

EARLY CHRISTIANITY IN UKRAINE

Pre-Christian Ukrainians (the people of Kievan Rus) were pagans. Their beliefs were informed by the powers of nature, and gods were representations of nature's various elements: wind, rain, frost, and so forth. In a country with long, cold winters, the god of the sun was the most powerful. If appropriately worshipped, the gods had the ability to bestow fertility, sunshine, wealth, and health. When defied, however, the gods sent drought, disease, and war. Reflections of some pagan beliefs can still be found in many Christian traditions.

Christianity made its way to Kievan Rus almost immediately after the state was formed, in the seventh century. Small groups of the population exposed to the influences of the Byzantine Empire adopted Christianity in the eighth and ninth centuries. The presence of Christian military men from

Constantinople in 860 hastened the spread of the religion, adding to the number of believers.

Only a century later, in 988, Prince Volodymyr the Great adopted Christianity as the official religion for Kievan Rus. His decision was dictated by the growing popularity of Christianity in Europe, and the need to integrate Kievan Rus into the cultural, political, and economic life of the West. It was the Greek branch of Christianity that prevailed and became the model on which Ukrainian and Russian Christianity were based for centuries to come.

Nonetheless, the transition from pagan to Christian beliefs was not a smooth one. Russian chronicles tell of a crowd of Kiev's inhabitants driven forcibly by soldiers to the Dnieper River and baptized there en masse. Statues of pagan gods were dismantled, burned, or thrown into the Dnieper. Many names in modern Kiev reflect the events of those days. For example, the main street in Kiev is *Hreschatyk* (hreh-SCHAH-tik), a derivation of "to cross," or "to baptize," because it was the route by which the pagan crowd was herded to the river. Another part of the city is called *Holosiyivka* (hoh-loh-SIH-iv-kah), from the Ukrainian "to weep," because it was there that those who managed to escape from the forced baptism grieved for their banished gods.

SOVIET YEARS

Under communism, the Soviet government aimed to eliminate religion in favor of a state-sponsored atheism. Many church properties—like all private property—were confiscated by the state and either destroyed or used for other purposes. Some churches or cathedrals were made into museums. Although many Orthodox priests and faithful were executed, tortured, imprisoned, exiled, or harassed by Soviet authorities, the church itself was never completely banned. However, any sort of educational groups, schools, or publications were illegal. Various Soviet leaders throughout the twentieth century either encouraged the church—for ethnic patriotic reasons—or quashed it, based on whatever served their own political needs at the time.

WHAT IS ORTHODOX?

Orthodox means "traditionally accepted as right or true." In Christian churches, it usually means the doctrine has remained pure and unchanged over time.

This emphasis on tradition is evident in the Orthodox church services. The order in which a church service progresses is the same as it has been for centuries. The sermon must always come from the holy books of the Bible. The musical liturgy of the choir has been fixed for every occasion and cannot be chosen randomly. This music is very specific and can only be heard in Orthodox churches. No musical instruments are allowed, and laughter, or even smiling, is prohibited—praying to God is a very serious matter.

There are a number of small rules of correct behavior that are absent in many other churches. For example, the proper way for Orthodox Christians to cross themselves, to way to light a candle—only from other candles, never with a lighter or matches, the way to place one's hands—never behind one's back, and never in the pockets, and many others. Ukrainian Orthodox women always cover their heads with kerchiefs when they attend church.

JEWS

During World War II, about half the Jews living in Ukraine were murdered by the Germans. During Ukraine's years as part of the Soviet Union, Jewish cultural and religious life was harshly repressed. So it might be surprising that today, Jews in Ukraine make up the third-largest Jewish community in Europe and the fifth-largest in the world. Jews live mainly in Kiev, Dnepropetrovsk, Kharkov, and Odessa, as well as in many of the smaller towns. Nevertheless, Jews comprise a mere 0.2 percent of Ukraine's population.

Since Ukrainian independence in 1991, Jewish communities in the country have been revitalized and are generally well treated by the government. However, the Jewish population is declining as it ages and many elderly Jews live in poverty. Younger people opt to move to Israel for better economic opportunity. Since 1989, about two hundred thousand Ukrainian Jews have emigrated to Israel.

CHRISTIAN ARCHITECTURE

Constantinople sent missionaries to help Kievan Rus establish Christianity. Byzantine priests taught Kievan volunteers, who became the first Kievan priests. Byzantine architects taught Kievan master builders to erect Christian churches, which is when the beautiful onion-domed cathedrals first appeared in Kiev, Novgorod, Volodymyr, and many other cities of Kievan Rus.

The first cathedrals were needed as soon as possible, so they were built of wood and covered with shingles. The typical feature in all Orthodox churches, ancient and modern, is the tripartite construction: a vestibule, or entrance hall, located in the west, a sanctuary in the east—the sanctuary is the part of the church where only the priest and his assistants are admitted, and the main congregational area in between. The tradition of building bell towers separately from the churches originated so as not to overload the wooden structures.

As architecture became more sophisticated, brick and stone churches were built often with several chapels surrounding the central room. A church was always constructed in the form of a cross, no matter how many parts it consisted of. Unlike many other churches, Ukrainian Orthodox churches do not have any pews, and those who come to worship either stand or kneel on the hard floor during services.

Ukrainian baroque churches were built using a unique style of church architecture, sometimes called Cossack architecture, because it was used between the mid-seventeenth and eighteenth centuries, the time of the most active Cossack movement. Architecturally, Ukrainian Cossack churches are a blend of Byzantine and western European influences. Cossack churches were made all of wood, the parts joined meticulously without a single nail. Only a few have survived the misfortunes of time: floods, fires, and vandalism. They can be seen in central Ukraine, not far from Kiev, Chernihiv, and Cherkasy.

MUSLIMS

Sources differ considerably, but in 2012, the US State Department estimated Ukraine's Muslim population at about five hundred thousand. Of those, about three hundred thousand were Crimean Tatars.

During the Soviet era, Joseph Stalin accused the Tatar people of collaborating with the Nazis during World War II. He decided to clear the entire population of ethnic Tatars from Crimea, and deported them to Soviet Uzbekistan, a primarily Muslim republic in the Soviet Union. Along the way, many thousands died of starvation or disease in what Ukraine's parliament has officially recognized as genocide.

In recent years, many Tatars have returned home to Crimea—albeit to find themselves once again under Russian rule since the 2014 annexation. In 2017, Ukraine asked the United Nations to assess the status of freedom of religion and belief on Crimea since the Russian takeover.

RELIGION TODAY

After the collapse of the Soviet Union, Orthodox Christianity was revitalized. Many people who grew up under the Soviet system looked to the church to salvage some their Ukrainian heritage. Religion returned to homes and neighborhoods in the form of icons and restored churches. In 1988, even before Ukraine's official independence, Kiev attracted thousands of visitors for the celebration of the Millennium of Christianity in Rus at Kiev Pechersk Lavra (the Cave Monastery), despite the fact that at the time it was still labeled as a museum.

For the younger generation, the return to religion has become a popular trend. What once was considered old-fashioned behavior and denounced by the Communist youth, is today not only condoned, it has been embraced by droves of young Ukrainians. The Orthodox Church is so influential that its representatives can be found in parliament, local legislatures, electoral campaigns, and even in the army.

Kiev Pechersk Lavra (KIH-ih peh-CHER-sk LAH-vrah) is the oldest monastery in Ukraine, built at the dawn of the Christian era in Kievan Rus. The word pechera *means "cave." The term* lavra *is reserved for the highest-ranking monasteries of the Eastern Orthodox Church. Besides Kiev Pechersk, only one other monastery in western Ukraine has gained the status of lavra.*

Just as Mecca is a sacred place for Muslims to visit at least once in their lifetime, Kievo-Pecherska Lavra in Kiev has become a sacred place for all Orthodox Christians. The monastery consists of numerous churches, a huge bell tower, dormitories, a maze of caves, underground rooms, and connecting corridors. The original caves were excavated in the eleventh century and served not only as places to hide from invaders but also as places to meditate in solitude, isolated from the cruelty and noise of the outside world.

Since 1990, the monastery, along with the Saint Sophia Cathedral in the historic center of Kiev, has been designated a UNESCO World Heritage Site.

INTERNET LINKS

http://church.ua/en
The site of the Ukrainian Orthodox Church, Moscow Patriarchate, is partly translated into English.

http://risu.org.ua/en/index
The Religious Information Service of Ukraine reports up-to-date religious news in English.

LANGUAGE

Books of *Harry Potter and the Cursed Child*, translated into Ukrainian, are displayed in Kiev.

9

WHEN UKRAINE WAS PART OF THE Soviet Union, the official language was Russian. That meant that all business correspondence, official communications, and printed newspapers were in Russian. National radio stations and television channels were broadcast solely in Russian, and although the Ukrainian mass media were permitted to operate (to some degree), they were much less influential and pervasive than their Russian counterparts.

One of the first things Ukraine did upon winning its independence was to reinstate Ukrainian as the official language. However, the problem of language is not that simple a matter to resolve. Years of Russification had a tremendous influence on the Ukrainian people. Today, many Ukrainians speak better Russian than their own Ukrainian, having grown up using Russian in school.

In fact, Russian and Ukrainian are very closely related languages, with a 60 percent shared vocabulary. Nevertheless, for many Ukrainians, having their own language restored as the national language is a matter of national pride more than an issue of literacy.

Ukrainian is the country's only official, nationwide language. However, according to legislation passed in 2012, a language spoken by at least 10 percent of an oblast's population is given the status of a "regional language," allowing for its use in courts, schools, and other government institutions.

UKRAINIAN

Ukrainian belongs to the large family of Indo-European languages, along with English, Spanish, and many other modern languages. At the same time, Ukrainian also belongs to the Slavic branch, along with Polish, Bulgarian, and Russian, while English is on the Germanic branch, along with German and Dutch. Therefore, although the Ukrainian and English languages are related, their kinship is rather a distant one.

The relationship, however, is evident in certain words. For example, "two" and "three" in English are *dva* (di-VA) and *try* (tree) in Ukrainian; the English word "beat" is *byty* (BIT-tea) in Ukrainian; and "water" translates as *voda* (VO-da). There are many other words that only comparative linguistics can identify as being related. In some cases it's not clear whether a word has the same origin or was just borrowed from another language (compare the English word "hut" with the Ukrainian *khata* [CA-ta], the meaning in both languages is approximately the same thing). There are very few words in the English language borrowed from the Ukrainian, but there are many words in Ukrainian that are from English.

Words representing specific activities or items originating in foreign cultures in the last century, such as "jazz," "jeans," "computer," and "rock and roll," have been adopted without any changes. There are also words that sound almost identical but mean quite different things, to the confusion of inexperienced translators. For example, the Ukrainian *mahazyn* (ma-ha-ZEEN) means "store," not "magazine."

WRITTEN UKRAINIAN

At the end of the eleventh century, the Slavic languages began to exhibit distinct differences from each other. This is usually explained by migration and cultural influences from neighboring countries.

The written Ukrainian language originated in the ninth century, when the Byzantine missionary brothers Saint Cyril and Saint Methodius created an alphabet based on Greek and Hebrew letters. This system of characters

developed into what is called the Cyrillic alphabet, after Saint Cyril. The Cyrillic alphabet, used by scholarly missionaries to translate the Bible into the Slavic language, is still used today, with some adaptations, by Ukrainians, Russians, Belarussians, Bulgarians, and other Slavic nations.

The sign outside the United States Embassy in Kiev displays both English and Ukrainian.

The Ukrainian alphabet has thirty-three letters. One letter, Ð, the soft sign—called the front *yer*—does not have its own sound, but makes the preceding consonant "soft," thus changing its pronunciation. There are two features of Ukrainian that make it easy for an English speaker to learn: the letters are pronounced exactly the way they are pronounced in the alphabet, regardless of their accented or unaccented position in the word, and the structure of the sentence (syntax) is more flexible than in English, allowing wide stylistic leeway.

MEDIA

In a famous Ukrainian joke, a member of an inspection committee asks a randomly picked person in the streets of Kiev, "Do you have everything that you need?" "Yes." "Can you buy everything in state stores?" "Sure." "Do you read newspapers?" "Of course—how else would I know that I have everything I need?"

The joke illustrates the ridiculous difference between what was written in newspapers and the actual situation in Ukraine before independence. All mass media were state-owned and state-supported. Reporters' material was thoroughly censored by editors who were appointed to their positions and strictly supervised by the Communist Party committee. No matter what happened in the country, news was always rosy. The most one could find out about a plane crash, if anything at all, was something like "there were victims." A disaster the size of the Chernobyl nuclear power plant explosion was not mentioned in the press at all. To keep control over such powerful mass media as television and radio, the central leadership prohibited the development of local television stations. Thus there were only two television channels from Moscow and one or two from Kiev available in Ukraine. Crammed with propaganda, the national channels' advantage was the complete absence of commercial advertising. The same was true for radio.

The evolution of private electronic mass media has been slowed by provisions in the Law on Television and Radio Broadcasting that was enacted by parliament in 1994. Constant personnel changes in the State Committee on Television and Radio Broadcasting have caused bureaucratic delays as well. According to new laws, priority will be given to stations promoting Ukrainian culture and language. The law requires all private television and radio stations to broadcast a minimum of 50 percent domestic content, as opposed to devoting full airtime to powerful satellite services, such as Voice of America or the BBC.

Freedom of the press and electronic mass media is guaranteed by the Ukrainian constitution, a surety that has produced unexpected results. As more and more of newly created print newspapers appeared on the streets (private radio and television developed more slowly), standards and quality fell below what was previously judged as acceptable.

Press freedom has improved since the 2004 Orange Revolution, and there is decreased government intervention in the work of journalists. Their work, however, is still being hampered by the real and persistent threat of injury and even murder. Here are several examples (there are numerous others):

In 2001, Oleh Breus, the publisher of *XXI Vek*—a regional weekly—was shot dead by two gunmen outside his home in Luhansk.

In the same year, Ihor Oleksandrov, director of the private television and radio station TOR in Slavyansk, died after four unidentified men attacked him at his office. Oleksandrov's death was believed to be linked to his investigations into corruption and organized crime. (In 2012, four former policemen were sentenced to seven to thirteen years in prison for fraud in the criminal case involving Oleksandrov.)

In 2004, the director of Radio Yuta in Poltava, Yuriy Chechyk, died in a dubious car crash while on his way to a meeting with executives of Radio Liberty's Ukrainian Service.

In 2014, the prominent crime reporter Aleksander Kuchinsky and his wife were murdered in their country home in Eastern Ukraine.

And in 2015, Oles Buzina, a leading Ukrainian journalist known for his pro-Russian views, was shot dead in Kiev by two masked gunmen.

In 2016, Freedom House, an independent watchdog organization, ranked Ukraine's press freedom as "partly free." State interference in media affairs had decreased drastically since the Euromaidan protests and the ouster of President Viktor Yanukovych in 2014, the report said. However, the government's fraught relationship with Russia, not to mention the extreme danger to journalists in the separatist-held regions, has had a dampening effect on press freedom.

DIALECTS AND NONVERBAL COMMUNICATION

Some of the peculiarities in pronunciation and vocabulary make it easy to distinguish a person from the Poltava area in central Ukraine from his counterpart in the western part of Ukraine, and a person who grew up in the south from one who lives in the east. Subjected to continuous invasions and numerous outside influences, Ukrainians in these areas have developed very distinctive dialects. Of course, not everyone in these regions uses the same language patterns, and a standard Ukrainian speech is used by the media and taught in schools, so there are rarely any problems of miscommunication.

Gestures and instinctive reactions also figure prominently in communication. Ukrainians use their hands, movements of the head, and facial expressions to emphasize the meaning of their words. Some gestures are common outside Ukraine as well, for example, the slight nodding of one's head while listening to a conversation (meaning "I comprehend and agree"); shaking one's head from left to right (meaning "I disagree"); or clapping one's hands (signifying approval and encouragement). Others are unique to Ukraine, such as whistling during concerts and performances to convey disapproval.

FORMS OF ADDRESS

Since 1921 when the Ukrainian Soviet Socialist Republic was established, the terms "Mr." and "Mrs." in Ukraine were supplanted by the genderless "comrade." The explanation was that under Communism everyone is meant to be equal. Today the traditional *pan* (pahn) for Mr., *pani* (PAH-nih) for Mrs., and *panna* (PAH-nah) for Miss are gradually replacing comrade. Which form of address is the appropriate one, however, is temporarily a puzzle for Ukrainians, who, to avoid any bias, quite often use no salutation at all in letters besides the name.

There are two ways to say "you" in Ukrainian: the formal vy and the familiar *ty*. The second, as a rule, is used between people who address each other by their first names, which does not happen as readily in Ukraine as it does in North America. It is rude to call someone by only their first or last name if it is the first meeting. The first name in combination with the patronymic name is the best approach. For example, Ivan Mykolayovych is the appropriate way to address a man whose father's last name was Mykolayovy, or Tetyana Petrivna for a woman whose father's name was Petriv.

INTERNET LINKS

https://freedomhouse.org/report/freedom-press/2016/ukraine
Freedom House evaluates the world's countries according to their freedom of the press and other freedoms.

http://www.omniglot.com/writing/ukrainian.htm
Omniglot provides a basic introduction to Ukrainian, along with many links, useful phrases, and audio files.

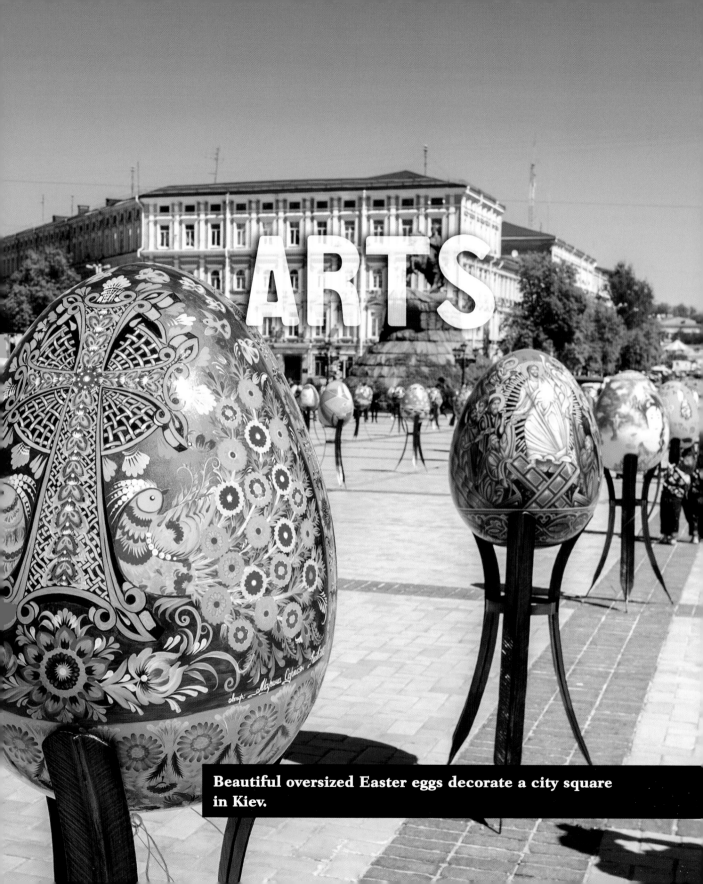

ARTS

Beautiful oversized Easter eggs decorate a city square in Kiev.

10

THE ARTS IN UKRAINE RANGE FROM the humble to the glorious. The embroidery on a simple dishcloth, the decoration on an Easter egg, or the tinkling of the lute-like bandura are as central to Ukrainian culture as the great golden domes of St. Michael's Monastery in Kiev. Decorative ornamental arts and crafts are especially rich traditions with roots that go far back into history.

The Ukrainian singer, songwriter and actress Jamala (b. 1983) won the 2016 Eurovision Song Contest with her song "1944." It describes the deportation of the Crimean Tatars in the 1940s by the Soviet Union, and in particular, relates her great-grandmother's experience of losing her young daughter while being deported to Central Asia.

The golden domes of St. Michael's Monastery gleam in the sunshine.

An old Ukrainian folk glass icon

Two main forces drove the development of art in Ukraine: service to God and the desire to express emotion through decoration and depiction of the environment. Popular motifs were derived from the various stages in Ukraine's history. From the mysterious Trypillyan culture came the spiral, repeated again and again as a symbol of the ongoing creation of life; circles represented the sun, the most important of the pagan gods; crosses were embroidered in cloth to guard and protect the name of the Savior. Foreign conquerors attempted to suppress these art forms, but the oppression only strengthened the folk art movement as an expression of national identity.

RELIGIOUS ICONS

Service to God in art is characterized best of all by a variety of church icons, which are small religious paintings. Icons play an important role in Eastern Orthodox Christianity. More than just decorations, they are depictions of Jesus, the saints, or scenes from the Gospels, and are considered to be sacred conduits to God. Every aspect of an icon is symbolic, from its design to its colors.

To make an icon, a wooden panel is sanded down until the surface is clean and smooth. The paints were traditionally made from a base of egg yolks and other natural ingredients. The oldest surviving icons in Ukraine, painted in the eleventh century, depict events in the Bible and saints in Eastern Orthodox history. These early paintings can be seen at Kiev's Saint Sofia Cathedral.

The craft of the *bohomaz* (boh-hoh-MAHZ), as the artists were called, was well respected, but contrary to popular belief, the artists themselves were not. In fact, very often they were serfs working for a landlord who would permit them to contract work with churches and give them only a small share of the payment collected.

PYSANKY-UKRAINIAN EASTER EGGS

The art of decorating eggs in the spring has become associated with Easter over the years, but this art form existed long before Christianity came to Ukraine. In many countries around the world, spring is a celebration of new life, and Ukrainians believe there is a great power in the new life embodied in an egg. Ancient legends of many cultures tell of a giant egg from which the universe emerged. Eggs were believed to have the power to heal, protect, and to bring good luck and wealth. Such beliefs are the reason behind the tradition of keeping a plateful of decorated eggs in the home.

After the introduction of Christianity to Ukraine, the art of egg decorating continued to develop. Today there are two types of decorated Easter eggs. The simpler one, called krashanka *(KRAH-shahn-kah), is an edible hard-cooked egg painted with one bright color. The more detailed* pysanka *(PIH-sahn-kah) is made from a raw, empty egg shell, painted with various colors and designs, and kept in the house as decoration.*

The long, careful procedure used in making pysanka eggs is one of the things that makes them so beautiful. The design is drawn in melted wax on the surface of the egg. Then the egg is dipped in different colored dyes, from brightest to darkest, with new wax being applied between dippings. The wax pattern seals the color, so it will resist the dye bath. Before the final step, the egg is heavily coated with wax. But when the wax is heated and wiped from the egg, the miracle of the artist's creation is revealed.

Traditionally, the dyes were made of various herbs and plants, including sunflower seeds, walnuts, buckwheat husks, moss, and birch leaves. Today, the dyes can be bought as powder and mixed as desired. The kistka *(KIST-kah), or stylus, the tool used for drawing the wax pattern has also been updated. In the old days, the stylus was filled with wax and then had to be warmed by the flame of a candle every minute to ensure that the wax did not cool. Now there are electric styluses of various sizes that, when plugged in, keep the wax hot.*

Celebrants wear traditional embroidered white blouses in a folk dress parade in Kiev.

EMBROIDERY

For hundreds of years, Ukrainian women have devoted long winter nights to weaving, embroidering, and attaching complicated bead designs to their clothing. Traditionally, mothers and their daughters embroidered a shirt, handkerchief, or tobacco pouch for their husbands, sons, or sweethearts. Floral designs were embroidered on towels and napkins that were hung in the kitchen and throughout the house. Embroidery can also be found in the interior of churches on altar cloths and hangings, and in priests' vestments. Wedding dresses are still intricately hand embroidered.

Embroidery is a long process demanding time and patience. Different parts of the country have their own unique patterns, but black and red threads against a white background are the prevailing colors throughout the land. "Red for love, black for sorrow"—red and black are traditional colors in many fields of Ukrainian art, representing life's polarities.

MUSIC

Ukrainian is a very melodious language. But the "singsong" sound of the language only partially explains why Ukrainians like to sing so much. Music is inevitably a part of any party or get-together, used to express both joy and sorrow.

Ukrainian music developed from a basis of folk songs, many of them composed and spread by *kobzars* (kob-ZAHRS), bards who traveled from town to town performing their music. The name *kobzar* was derived from the name of the musical instrument they used to accompany their songs. The *kobza* is an ancient Ukrainian instrument (very much like a round lute with three or four strings), a predecessor of the *bandura* (bahn-DOO-rah), another stringed musical instrument. The bandura, which is asymmetrical in shape and contains up to sixty strings, became popular in the seventeenth century. In the Carpathian Mountains one can also play the trembita (trem-BEE-tah),

Musicians called bandurists play beautiful, full-sized banduras during a concert in Lviv in 2017.

An old man in folk-style clothing plays a trembita in the mountains.

a wind instrument with a profoundly mournful sound. Made in the shape of a cylindrical tube, trembitas can be as long as 10 feet (3 m).

Unlike in other countries, Ukrainian folk music had not, until recently, merged with pop music. There have been several attempts in recent years to create a uniquely Ukrainian rock-and-roll genre, and one success story is found in Ruslana Lyzhychko (b. 1973). Known professionally by only her first name, Ruslana won the Eurovision song contest in 2004 with her inspiring mix of traditional Ukrainian music and modern rock. She went on to become singer, songwriter, producer, musical conductor, multi-instrumentalist, dancer, voice actress, and social activist. She became a politician and served in the Ukrainian parliament.

Some of the most famous Ukrainian folk singers are Nina Matviyenko, Raisa Kyrychenko, and Anatoliy Solovianenko. Mykola Lysenko, a passionate promoter of Ukrainian music, and Mykola Leontovych, the composer of the world-famous "Carol of the Bells," are other well-known Ukrainian musicians.

DANCE

Dance, as a form of art or simply as entertainment, is very popular in Ukraine. Folk dances vary in style, depending on the region. In the west, group dances made up of both men and women are popular. The ritual meanings of the dances have been lost in time, and today they are usually danced to commemorate important events—especially weddings—and to entertain the public.

What is known to the world as Cossack dancing indeed originated with the Cossacks of the sixteenth century but not as a dance at all. The vigorous movements were part of a regime of calisthenics to keep the Cossacks fit for battle. Not until much later was the discipline transformed into a group dance with leaps, rapid movements, and comic improvisations. This dance is called the *hopak* (hoh-PAHK), or "the Cossack Dance," and it can be performed only by very well-trained artists.

INTERNET LINKS

http://euromaidanpress.com/2016/05/19/secret-ancestral-codes-12-main-symbols-in-ukrainian-embroidery
This illustrated article explains the meanings behind various embroidery designs.

http://www.rusmoose.com/traditional-ukrainian-dance
This Russian site offers videos of many kinds of Ukrainian dances.

http://www.startribune.com/ukrainian-easter-eggs-come-to-life-in-hands-of-minn-woman-91/298919271/#6
This 2015 article includes a slide show and video about a Ukrainian American pysanky artist.

http://time.com/4329061/eurovision-jamala-russian-ukraine-crimea
This article explains the lyrics to Jamala's hit song "1944."

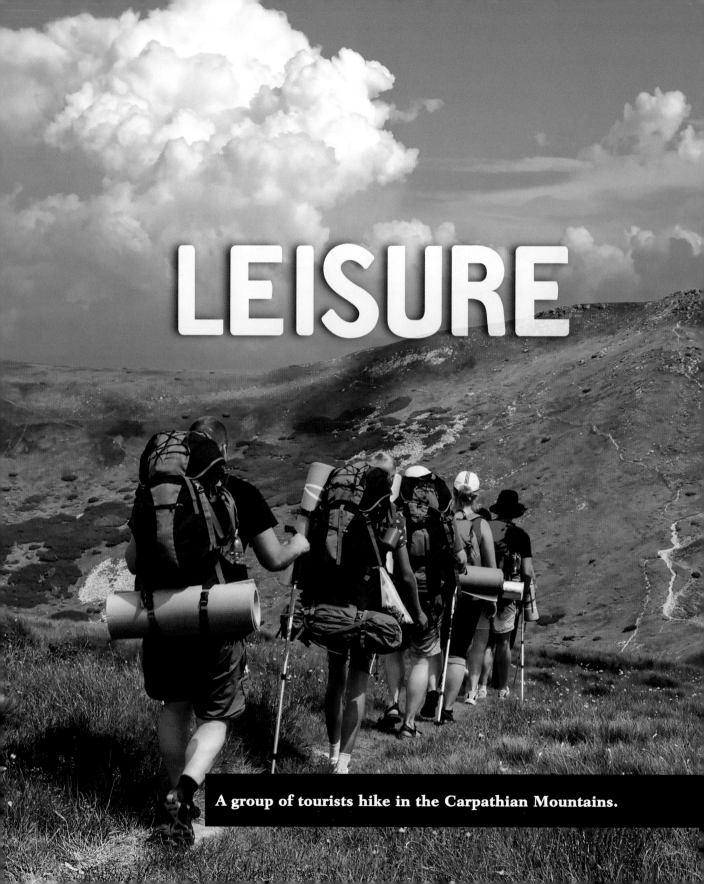

LEISURE

A group of tourists hike in the Carpathian Mountains.

11

UKRAINIANS SPEND THEIR FREE TIME carefully, making the most of time off. Picnics are a popular way of combining the relaxation of eating, drinking, singing, and getting fresh air. Movies, plays, and ballet are great weekend activities if tickets are available. Prices for excellent classical concerts, operas, and stage productions are relatively inexpensive, often priced at just a few dollars even at the National Opera in Kiev.

Unfortunately, as in many places, weekends are most often the only time for people to take care of chores at home. That is why for many people painting, gardening, laundry, cleaning, and general household maintenance and repairs have become leisure activities.

AT HOME

There are folks in Ukraine who could easily qualify as "couch potatoes," with only one difference—it is not so much that they are chained to the couch but that they have a love of the home in general. "Let's get together on Saturday, our place," is a typical weekend invitation that is extended spontaneously to a friend during a telephone conversation on Friday. The invitation is usually accepted or rejected on the spot. For Ukrainians, eating is a form of leisure. Having a meal is not just a way to

Use of the internet continues to grow in Ukraine, where about 49 percent of the people had internet access in 2015. That figure is up from 43 percent in 2014 and 41 percent in 2013. However, the conflicts in the separatist-dominated East and Russian-occupied Crimea have affected internet freedom. Rebels and Russian authorities have blocked certain Ukrainian internet service providers and other communication services.

Crowds of people gather around outdoor tables during Kiev's Street Food Festival in April 2016.

satisfy one's hunger, it is also a time to chat with friends and family about the day's events or the political situation. Relatives may often get together for dinner once or twice a week, with the whole family pitching in to help with the food arrangements.

Spending evenings in front of the television—or increasingly, the computer—has become routine leisure for many Ukrainian families. Recently, a few international channels and substantially more specialized cable channels have become available. Parents are becoming concerned about their children's leisure time, because watching television competes with friends, homework, reading, and outdoor play for their attention.

Today, newspapers provide as much choice in entertainment as television does. There are dozens of different papers dedicated to a wide variety of topics, from politics to sports.

SPORTS

Sports complexes are found in every large city in Ukraine. These complexes usually house a swimming pool and facilities for aerobics, boxing, and team games. For students, there are sports academies or their own secondary school facilities. If nothing else is available, simply a flat grassy surface somewhere in a park will work well for soccer games.

Adults are also taking part in amateur sports competitions. The most popular amateur sports are soccer, basketball, volleyball, hockey, and boxing. Tennis is slowly making its way to Ukraine and, more recently, martial arts such as karate and kung fu. Golfers will be disappointed that there is only one major golf course in the whole country, although there are lesser ones associated with hotels.

Ukrainian athletes were some of the strongest members of the Soviet Olympic teams. Some of these athletes gained worldwide recognition, such as pole vaulter Sergey Bubka and gymnasts Larisa Latynina and Hrihoriy Misyutin, to name only a few. Bubka went on to become president of the National Olympic Committee of Ukraine.

Since independence, Ukrainian athletes have brought honor to their own country. Ukrainians have traditionally been strong in the fighting sports. Today they are proud of their world-class professional boxers, especially the brothers Vitali Klitschko and Vladimir Klitschko. Figure skaters Oksana Baiul and Viktor Petrenko won Olympic medals in the 1990s. In more recent years,

The Ukrainian boxing champions, brothers Vladimir and Vitali Klitschko, show off their championship belts.

gymnast Oleg Vernyayev has become the country's top medal winner.

Soccer is the national sport of Ukraine, and there are many Ukrainian international soccer stars, notably Andriy Shevchenko, who played on the AC Milan team before his retirement in 2012. In 2006, for the first time in its football (as soccer is called) history, Ukraine qualified for the FIFA (International Federation of Association Football) World Cup in Germany and made it to the semifinals of that tournament. Many young Ukrainian boys dream of becoming famous soccer players on the Kiev Dynamo team. On the day of the final game in a championship match, all regular activity comes to a halt while fans nationwide watch the action on TV or listen to the coverage on the radio.

Cycling is also a popular pastime. For many people living in towns, bicycles are a means of transportation, especially appreciated in the days of fuel shortages. More serious cyclists participate in organized bicycle marathons. Though there are few special bicycle paths and trails, the traffic in Ukraine is fairly light, which makes cycling on city streets a safe and convenient way to travel and get some exercise at the same time.

A traditional marathon takes place in Odessa every year, dedicated to the anniversary of the city's liberation in 1944 from Nazi occupation during World War II. The participants follow a route, called the Circle of Glory, or Feodosiya, that passes by each of the monuments to the defenders of the city. People of all ages take part in patriotic shared events like this one.

TRAVEL

Vacation time begins as soon as the weather turns warm, usually from the middle of May until the middle of August. Some Ukrainians plan their vacations ahead of time by booking a tour package through a travel agency. Other people go to resorts by the sea or take what are called "wild" vacations in Ukraine, meaning they drive to their chosen destination, pitch a tent, and cook their food over a campfire. The absence of laws for private land ownership makes camping like this possible, but local governments in seaside towns do their best to keep the hordes of "wild" tourists to a minimum.

International destinations have long been the dream of many Ukrainian travelers. In the past, because of tight political repression and the lack of ready cash, such trips were destined to remain dreams. Ukrainians today are free to travel the world, but for the majority of the population, international travel is still too costly. One pleasant outcome of independence is that a large number of emigrants have come home to visit their relatives, which they couldn't do before.

ALONE WITH NATURE

Some people's idea of a perfect vacation is to escape the city crowds and surround themselves with nature. Though Ukraine is a densely populated country, it is still possible to find an isolated spot on the bank of a river or lake to fish, camp, and swim.

Others, desiring something more adventurous, find white-water rafting down Ukraine's major rivers a thrilling sport. During the summer months, elaborate rafts with single adventurers or whole families can be seen on the Dnister, Dnieper, or Privdenny Bug rivers.

For winter vacation enthusiasts, there are many resort areas, especially in the Carpathian Mountains. For those interested in skiing, there is no better place than Yaremcha in western Ukraine, renowned for its beauty, delicious food, and spas, not to mention the excellent ski slopes.

INTERNET LINKS

http://www.ffu.org.ua/eng
The Football (Soccer) Federation of Ukraine has an English language version of its website.

http://www.ukraine.com/activities
Ukraine's travel site offers information on various sports and activities.

FESTIVALS

Hardy souls plunge into icy waters in Cherkassy, Ukraine, as part of a traditional Epiphany ritual in January 2017.

12

H
OLIDAYS IN UKRAINE HAVE THEIR roots in several sources—history, culture, church, and politics. Like most countries, Ukraine celebrates its nationhood with patriotic festivals.

Constitution Day on June 28 commemorates the adoption of the newly-independent country's constitution in 1996. The day is celebrated with fireworks, parades, and musical events. Independence Day on August 24 is a similar, even grander, festival, marking Ukraine's 1991 liberation as a sovereign nation, free of the Soviet Union. It's a day for

Drummers perform at a Constitution Day celebration in Sumy, Ukraine.

One unusual festival that has emerged in recent years is Woodstock Ukraine. Produced by the charitable organization Heart to Heart, the annual gathering takes place in Lviv at the end of July. Inspired by the original 1969 Woodstock Music Festival in Bethel, New York, this outdoor fest focuses on peace, love, and music. Woodstock Ukraine has a strong antiwar message and features popular Ukrainian bands.

wearing traditional folk costumes and waving the Ukrainian flag. Fireworks, sports events, and plenty of outdoor fun are also typical.

When Ukraine left the Soviet Union, its calendar of holidays changed a good deal. During the Soviet years, political holidays were celebrated on the anniversaries of the Russian Revolution of 1917, on the date when the latest version of the constitution was adopted, and on May 1, as an expression of the solidarity of the working classes of the world. Religious holidays were not officially celebrated at all, but unofficially, people quietly observed them the way their ancestors had done for centuries. The holidays were listed on the church calendar, issued by the Ukrainian Orthodox patriarch's office every year.

All the changes in the political, economic, and cultural life of Ukrainians have been reflected in their holidays. Holidays with political significance to the former USSR are generally not celebrated anymore.

NEW YEAR

During the Soviet years when celebrating Christmas was prohibited, New Year became a very important holiday. In fact, today New Year is probably considered the biggest holiday of the year. Ukrainians put up New Year trees, which they decorate with ornaments. The trees came to be known as New Year trees because although they are decorated as if to celebrate Christmas, they are taken into the house only a few days before the new year and stand until January 13. This is a special day for some Ukrainians who still celebrate "Old New Year," the start of the new year according to the old calendar, abolished long ago by Peter the Great.

New Year is a time for family reunions, and people travel long distances to be with their relatives at this time of year. New Year is symbolic of the beginning of a new and better life, and even the wildest dreams are believed to come true on this day.

New Year's Eve is full of laughter, goodwill, and entertainment, with much eating, drinking, dancing, and playing of games. Many revelers celebrate throughout the night, and do not go to bed at all.

CHRISTMAS

Ukrainians celebrate Christmas on January 7, according to the traditions of the Eastern Orthodox calendar. On Christmas Eve, churches hold special services based on ancient rituals. The priests robe in colorful garments of silver and gold, and the choirs perform treasured old hymns. After the service, family members gather for a festive dinner of twelve traditional and symbolic dishes.

The week of January 7—14 is a festive week full of caroling, concerts, and visiting. The tradition of Christmas caroling is a long one. The prerevolutionary tradition was to present the carolers with sausages and bread and a shot of *horilka* (hoh-RIL-kah), Ukrainian vodka. Today, caroling is still alive and well in Ukraine, and long before Christmas Eve people make sure there are enough cookies, candies, and small coins for all the carolers. Greetings from the visiting group can be in the form of a short poem or song wishing household members happiness and health.

A Christmas Day celebration on January 7 in Transcarpathia, Ukraine

These days it is difficult to believe that it was only a few years ago that all religious holidays were officially prohibited. Older people still remember the circles of activists who surrounded churches on Christmas Eve to prevent children (who were forced to be members of the Young Communist League) from watching the service.

INTERNATIONAL WOMEN'S DAY

March 8 is a holiday for all women, mothers first and foremost. The holiday was established by a German Communist Party leader named Clara Zetkin to commemorate the struggle for women's rights. Over the years much of its political meaning has faded, and today it is comparable to Mother's Day in other countries. Husbands, boyfriends, fathers, and sons do their best to make this day as enjoyable as possible for women. Most families try to do something special for mother by preparing a special dinner, making a card, or giving her flowers. International Women's Day is a national holiday in Ukraine.

Men and women march to protest violence against women on International Women's Day in Kiev.

REMEMBERING THE WAR

Many people are puzzled when they see the size of World War II memorials in Ukraine. In Kiev, for example, the monumental statue of Mother Motherland, a woman holding a sword, is a part of the Museum of The History of Ukraine in World War II. The 203-foot- (62 m) tall steel statue symbolizes the country ready to defend itself. The Motherland character holds a shield bearing the national emblem of the Soviet Union, as Ukraine was a part of the Soviet Union during WWII. Although the statue remains controversial today, the memory of war still haunts. Five million Ukrainians died in that war, a catastrophe that touched virtually every family in the country.

Victory Day, May 9, recalls the victory over Ukraine's Nazi oppressors during World War II and a tribute to the countless soldiers who gave their lives defending the Soviet Union. It is also an antiwar holiday, a moving reminder of the atrocities of war. Flowers are carried to memorials, which can be found in every city and village in Ukraine. Veterans wear their decorations and gather

The enormous Soviet-style Mother Motherland statue rises high in Kiev.

Although it is not a day off, Holy Trinity Day, also called Pentecost, is the most important religious holiday after Christmas and Easter. It is celebrated in June, when the trees are green and beautiful, and for this reason it is often called "the green holiday" or "Green Sunday." According to the scriptures, the Holy Spirit appeared before the apostles on the fiftieth day after Jesus Christ's resurrection and granted them the ability to speak all of the world's languages in order to preach the world over.

Friends and family visit one another on this day and enjoy festive meals. The interiors of homes are decorated with fresh green grass, fragrant herbs, and tree branches, symbolizing the flourishing of life.

together to share their memories. Once, only the veterans of the Soviet army took to the streets on this day, but since independence, veterans of the Ukrainian Liberation Army (who fought both the German and Soviet armies in western Ukraine) freely celebrate Victory Day. Today, younger people in uniforms, veterans of the war in Afghanistan, can be seen mingling with the Liberation Army veterans and the venerable veterans of World War II.

EASTER

Another important religious holiday is Easter. Preparations for the holiday begin forty days before Easter Sunday, on Ash Wednesday. The Lenten season is rather strict—the faithful do not eat meat or animal fat for forty days, and avoid cheese and oils for seven days before Easter Sunday. Everything at home must be cleaned and decorated for Easter, inside and out. There are several solemn pre-Easter church services, with the culmination on Easter Sunday. Each family brings a basket of food to the church on Sunday morning to be blessed with holy water by the priest. After the food has been blessed, everyone goes home to break the fast. On Easter Sunday it is customary to greet people with the words "Christ is risen" to which they answer, "He is risen, indeed!"

The weekend after Easter is a family memorial time. Families make their way to their ancestral burial plots, clean and arrange the area, spend a quiet moment in remembrance of their loved ones, and have a picnic. Burial sites often have benches and tables installed for this custom.

OTHER SPECIAL DAYS

Palm Sunday is the first day of Holy Week and the Sunday before Easter. In Ukraine, a Palm Sunday procession moves from a church where the palms are blessed to a church where the liturgies are sung.

A relatively new tradition is to celebrate the Day of the City. For some newer cities, like Odessa, which celebrated only its bicentennial in 1994, it is easy to calculate the day of its founding. For other cities, people must guess. For example, Kiev is thought to be 1,500 years old. Whether or not the date is correct, everyone enjoys the colorful annual festivals.

Other special days find their source in pre-Christian history. For example, Kupula Night, also called Ivan Kupala Day, marks the summer solstice or Midsummer time, even though its celebration on July 7 is a few weeks past the solstice. The day is a time for merriment, love, romance, and old Slavic fertility rites, but also weaves in religious elements relating to John the Baptist. Women wear wreaths of flowers and folkloric costumes, young people jump over bonfires in tests of courage, and children engage in water fights and pranks.

INTERNET LINKS

http://greentourua.com/ukrainian-holidays-and-traditions
Brief descriptions and colorful photos explain some of Ukraine's main holidays.

https://www.timeanddate.com/holidays/ukraine
This calendar site lists Ukraine's official holidays and observances according to the current calendar year.

FOOD

Colorful spices are displayed for sale at a market.

13

TRADITIONAL UKRAINIAN CUISINE shares much in common with other countries in Eastern Europe. Slavic people enjoy many of the same dishes, albeit with small regional differences that can elicit great pride. Many Ukrainian favorites have their origins in Polish, Russian, Turkish, and Austro-Hungarian cultures. The nation's foremost food, however, has its roots in Ukraine itself. That is none other than *borsch*, or borscht, a beet soup that is revered as a national icon.

Ukrainian meals tend to be quite labor-intensive. Fast food is a relatively unknown concept. Meal preparation that typically requires the mixing, rolling, cutting, filling, and folding of dozens of tiny filled pasta-like dumplings, for example—as only one small part of the meal—clearly depends on the household's cook being home for most of the day. As modern life edges its way into Ukrainian culture, as it does in the urban areas, this will naturally change, but Ukrainians will surely find a way to hold on to their beloved cuisine, just as they did during the Soviet years.

Despite its name, the famous dish Chicken Kiev–a breaded chicken cutlet filled with garlic herb butter–is not Ukrainian at all. Rather it is Russian by way of France, where it was originally made with veal. In the nineteenth-century, Parisian-trained Russian chefs recreated the ritzy entree with chicken, which was more affordable. Today, restaurants in Kiev serve it mainly because tourists expect to find it on the menu.

LEAN TIMES

There has never been an abundance of fruit in Ukraine, but apples, cherries, plums, and other fruits grown in temperate climates are readily available. The same is true of vegetables. During the Soviet years, choices of fresh produce were few. Imported fruits and vegetables were limited to Cuban oranges. In those days, most Ukrainians could only read of bananas, pineapples, and coconuts.

Today, however, almost every possible tropical fruit and vegetable is in their markets. Prices are high, though when domestic fruits, nuts, and vegetables are in season, they are "dirt cheap."

Because much of Ukraine's agricultural infrastructure is not developed enough to provide fresh produce year-round to more people, seasonal canning and preserving is very common. Jams, concentrated fruit drinks, tomatoes, cucumbers, and many other food items are pickled or canned to be consumed in winter and spring, a vital necessity in most Ukrainian households. Almost every house and apartment complex is equipped with a cellar or cabinet where jams and pickled vegetables are stored.

Jams and marmalades for sale at a market in Kiev.

BORSCH

Borsch *(or borscht), the national dish of Ukraine, is usually the first course served in a Ukrainian meal. There are many versions of the soup served throughout the country, which reflects the individuality of Ukrainians as well as their ingenuity. It can contain as many as twenty different ingredients, depending on the season, region, and personal preferences of the cook, but usually includes beets, cabbage, tomato, served with a dollop of* smetana *(sour cream). It can be meatless or prepared with a rich meat stock featuring either beef or smoked pork.*

Beets are the principal ingredient in borsch, giving the soup its distinctive color and pleasing aroma. Borsch originated as a one-pot meal and can be served hot or cold. At its most complex, it is a lavish Ukrainian specialty and at its most contemporary, an elegantly chilled consommé (a clear soup made from clarified meat stock that often includes vegetables). Ukrainian borsch is borsch at its most extravagant. It can take several days to prepare, is made in large amounts, and is a dish fit for a feast!

BREADBASKET

Bread holds a lofty position in Ukrainian culture and cuisine, and it's no mystery why. The country's rich soil, particularly in the southern steppe regions, is famously known as *chernozem*, or "black earth"—some of the most fertile in the world. That soil, along with the region's mild climate and abundant rain, is good for growing grains. Ukraine, with its vast fields of wheat and other grains, has long been known as "the breadbasket of Europe."

Grains are important in many traditional Ukrainian dishes, including *kutia,* a Christmas Eve pudding made with wheat berries, dried fruits, and nuts. Bread itself, however, is more than just sandwich food. (In fact, sandwiches aren't even a part of Ukraine cuisine.) Bread is incorporated into life's most important rituals and celebrations, from births to marriages to funerals. Bread plays a role in Ukrainian folktales and folk wisdom.

Everyday breads include peasant-style rye breads and black sourdoughs breads. For special occasions, however, there are different breads for different holidays, and they are often quite beautiful.

Breads in a myriad of traditional shapes are displayed for Independence Day.

Babka (in western Ukraine), or *paska* (in Eastern Ukraine), is a sweet, eggy bread that is associated with Easter. It's often made in cylindrical forms, baked with raisins and other dried fruit, and decorated with icing and colorful sprinkles.

Kolach is slightly sweet, braided yeast bread, sometimes shaped into a ring. This bread is made at Christmastime, when its triple braided strands represent the Holy Trinity. When it's placed on the table for the Christmas Eve feast, a round kolach might have a candle in its center.

Raw vareniki are ready to be boiled.

Pampushka are buns that can be sweet or savory. Garlic buns and garlic breads are very popular for both everyday and special occasions.

Korovai is a ring-shaped bread usually baked for weddings. Korovai can be elaborately decorated with dough shapes, such as birds, which have symbolic meanings.

FILLED AND STUFFED THINGS

Ukrainians particularly love foods stuffed with fillings. *Holubtsi* (hoh-loob-TSIH), are cabbage rolls stuffed with rice and ground beef, typically baked in a tomato sauce. *Varenyki* (vah-REH-nih-kih), sometimes called *pyrohy* are turnover-style dumplings—something like Polish pierogies or Italian ravioli—with potato, mushroom, ground meat, or sauerkraut fillings. They can also be served for dessert with cherry, prune, or sweet cheese fillings. Sour cream is a typical accompaniment to both savory and sweet varenyki. Other stuffed foods include *kruchenyky* and *zavyvantsi*, which are pork or beef rolls stuffed with mushrooms, onions, eggs, cheese or vegetables, and *nalysnyky*, which are sweet or savory filled crepes. Even the international favorite, chicken Kiev, is a chicken cutlet filled with garlic-parsley butter.

THE TWELVE DISHES OF CHRISTMAS

Christmas Eve dinner is, for many folks, the highlight of the holiday season. Since the Ukrainian Christmas is celebrated according to the Eastern Orthodox tradition, the day itself falls on January 7, but the traditional family feast occurs the night before.

Christmas Eve day is spent fasting in spiritual anticipation of the holy night, and the table is decorated with a sheaf of hay to commemorate the stable of Christ's birth. Like in some other European nations, the Ukrainian Christmas Eve, or Sviaty Vechir, dinner has no meat. Some people also abstain from milk, eggs, and other dairy foods for this meal. The feast features twelve dishes representing the twelve apostles.

The meal begins only after the first star of the evening appears. The first dish is kutia, *a cold, sweet, grain dish or pudding made of cooked wheat berries, honey, raisins, poppy seeds, chopped nuts, and dried apricots. Kutia is said to symbolize prosperity, peace and good health. This is typically followed by a hot bowl of meatless borsch, the popular beet soup. Little mushroom-filled dumplings called* vuška *("little ears"), which look similar to tortellini, are a favorite addition to the soup.*

The other traditional dishes are based on grains, fish, beets, mushrooms, cabbage, beans, and potatoes or rice, as well as fresh and dried fruits. They may include pickled fish and vegetable dishes, such as pickled herring, salmon, and mushrooms; filled dumplings, or turnovers, (varenyki) and cabbage rolls (holubsti); fried fish or fish balls, stewed fruit compote, and of course, Ukrainian Christmas bread (kolach). Dessert is often fried, yeasted, sugared donuts with fruit fillings (pampushky), or honey cake (medivnyk).

THE WHOLE HOG (OR COW)

As is often true among country people who can't afford to waste food, all cuts of an animal are used. Ukrainian home cooks make beef or pork liver, tongue, lungs, kidneys, brains, and even stewed bulls' tails, which are a rare delicacy. Hogs' trotters (pigs' feet) are widely used by cooks and homemakers to make jellied minced meat or aspic. Liver pie (ground liver mixed with fried onions and other ingredients, fried in the shape of pancakes, and arranged in layers) is also considered a tasty delicacy in the Ukrainian cuisine.

DRINKS

Coffee drinking is seasonal in Ukraine, partly because coffee is not a traditional regional drink, and also because it is not as affordable. Although coffee drinking has yet to fully infiltrate the Ukrainian market and lifestyle, it has been made more available to shoppers today and is served in virtually every café. Its increasing popularity has also led to an increased demand for instant coffee, especially among the more affluent. Tea is greatly preferred, but iced tea is a strange concept to Ukrainians, who cannot imagine drinking tea any other way than hot. Juices, particularly apple, cherry, birch, and apricot, are popular in the summer, as well as carbonated soft drinks and Russian *kvas* (a fermented bread drink).

INTERNET LINKS

http://www.foodbycountry.com/Spain-to-Zimbabwe-Cumulative-Index/Ukraine.html
This site provides an overview of Ukrainian cuisine with some recipes.

https://www.lonelyplanet.com/ukraine/travel-tips-and-articles/76526
"Ukraine's culinary delights" is an article on this travel site.

UKRAINIAN *BORSCH* (BEET SOUP)

This meatless version would be appropriate for a Ukrainian Christmas Eve feast, but it can be enjoyed anytime.

2 Tbsp olive oil
2—3 large beets*, peeled and grated
12 cups (3 liters) water or broth (vegetable, chicken, or beef), or more as needed
1 large onion, peeled and chopped
2 carrots, peeled and grated
3 Tbsp tomato paste
2 Tbsp lemon juice
2 potatoes, peeled and diced
1—2 bay leaves
salt, pepper to taste
½ medium cabbage, cored and shredded
2 Tbsp or more white vinegar, to taste
fresh parsley, chopped
sour cream
fresh dill, chopped

In a large soup pot, add oil and sauté beets, carrots, and onions over a medium heat for about 5 minutes. Stir in tomato paste and cook for another 5 minutes. Add water or broth and lemon juice and bring to a boil. Add potatoes, bay leaves, salt and pepper. Stir. Return to a boil, lower heat, cover pot, and simmer for about 30 minutes.

Add cabbage and simmer for about 30 more minutes, or until all vegetables are very soft. Add vinegar and adjust seasonings.

Stir in parsley and dill. Serve borsch with a dollop of sour cream, and sprinkle generously with dill.

*Caution: beets will stain hands and clothing. Use plastic gloves and an apron or towel.

SIRNIKI (UKRAINIAN CHEESE PANCAKES)

Traditionally, these cheese pancakes are made with a soft fresh cheese called *tvorog*. They are popular throughout Eastern Europe.

1 cup golden raisins
15 oz (about 2 cups) (450 g) farmer's cheese, pot cheese, dry cottage cheese, ricotta, or quark
4 large eggs
¾ cups (90 g) all-purpose flour, plus about ½ cup (60 g) more for dredging
3 Tbsp sugar

1 tsp vanilla
½ tsp salt
1 tsp baking soda
1 tsp white vinegar
3 Tbsp canola oil, vegetable oil, or light olive oil for each batch

In a medium bowl, soak raisins in hot water to soften.

In a large bowl or a food processor, mix together cheese, eggs, ¾ cup (90 g) flour, sugar, vanilla, and salt. In a small bowl, stir together add baking soda and vinegar. The mixture will bubble. Add it to the cheese mixture, mix well.

Drain the raisins and pat dry in a paper towel. Stir the raisins into the cheese mixture. Batter will be lumpy. Heat a large skillet over medium heat, add 3 Tbsp cooking oil.

Add ½ cup (60 g) flour to a shallow bowl or rimmed plate. Scoop a heaping tablespoon of the cheese mixture into the flour. Turn the batter to flour both sides. With well-floured hands, gently shape into a patty, and place directly into the hot skillet. Work quickly to fill the pan with several pancakes, without crowding.

Sauté until golden brown, about 3—4 minutes on each side, flipping once during cooking. If pancakes brown too quickly, turn down the heat. Transfer pancakes to a warmed plate. Pancakes should be crispy on the outside and soft and fluffy on the inside.

Serve with sour cream, fruit, jam, applesauce, honey, or powdered sugar.

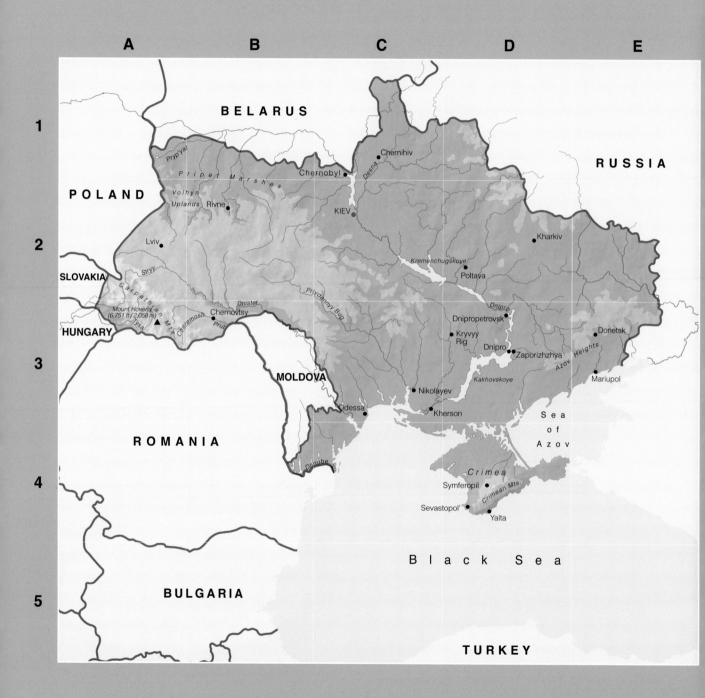

MAP OF UKRAINE

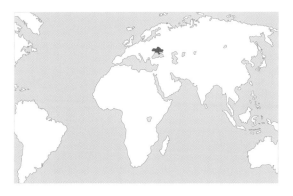

ECONOMIC UKRAINE

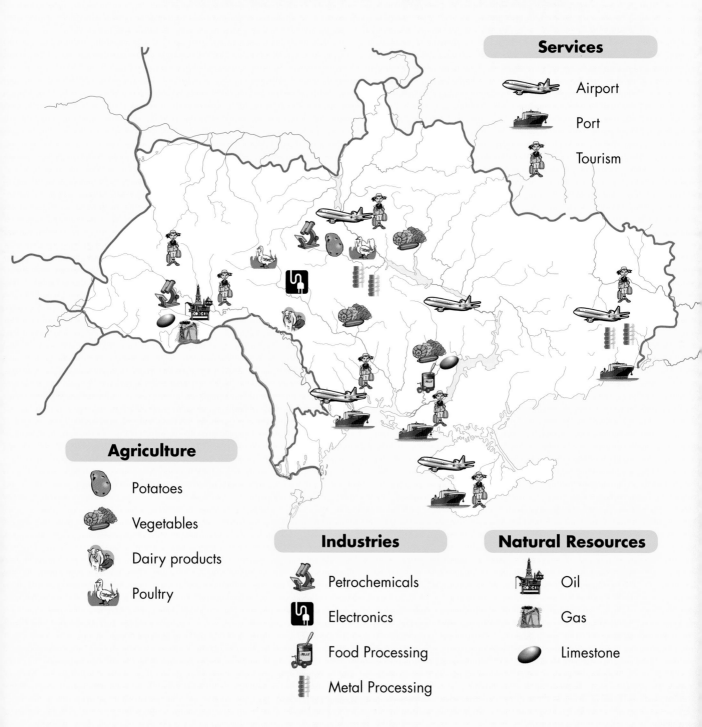

Services
- ✈ Airport
- 🚢 Port
- 🧍 Tourism

Agriculture
- 🥔 Potatoes
- 🥬 Vegetables
- 🐄 Dairy products
- 🐔 Poultry

Industries
- 🔬 Petrochemicals
- 🔌 Electronics
- Food Processing
- Metal Processing

Natural Resources
- Oil
- Gas
- Limestone

ABOUT THE ECONOMY

OVERVIEW

Russia's occupation of Crimea in 2014 and on-going aggression in eastern Ukraine have hurt economic growth. With the loss of a major portion of Ukraine's heavy industry in the Donbas and ongoing violence, Ukraine's economy shrunk by 6.8 percent in 2014 and by another 9.9 percent in 2015. Ukraine and Russia engaged in a trade war with sharply reduced trade between the countries. The EU-Ukraine Deep and Comprehensive Free Trade Area finally started up on January 1, 2016, and was expected to help Ukraine integrate its economy with Europe by opening up markets and harmonizing regulations.

GROSS DOMESTIC PRODUCT (GDP)

$87.2 billion (2015), official exchange rate

GDP SECTORS

Agriculture, 14.4 percent
Industry, 26.3 percent
Services, 59.3 percent (2016)

WORKFORCE

18 million (2016)

INFLATION RATE

13.5 percent (2016)

CURRENCY

Hryvnia (UAH)
USD 1 = 27.07 UAH (February 2017)
Notes: 1, 2, 5, 10, 20, 50, 100, 200, 500
1 hryvnya = 100 kopiykas
Coins (kopiykas): 1, 2, 5, 10, 25, 50

NATURAL RESOURCES

Iron ore, coal, manganese, natural gas, oil, salt, sulfur, graphite, titanium, magnesium, kaolin, nickel, mercury, timber, arable land

INDUSTRIAL PRODUCTS

Coal, electric power, ferrous and nonferrous metals, machinery and transport equipment, chemicals, food processing

AGRICULTURAL PRODUCTS

Grains, sugar beets, sunflower seeds, vegetables, beef, milk

UNEMPLOYMENT RATE

10 percent (2016)

POPULATION BELOW POVERTY LINE

24.1 percent (2010)

TRADE PARTNERS

EU, Turkey, China, Belarus, Poland, Egypt, Italy, Hungary

INTERNET ACCESSIBILITY

Internet users, 21.9 million
Percent of population, 49.3 percent(2015)

CULTURAL UKRAINE

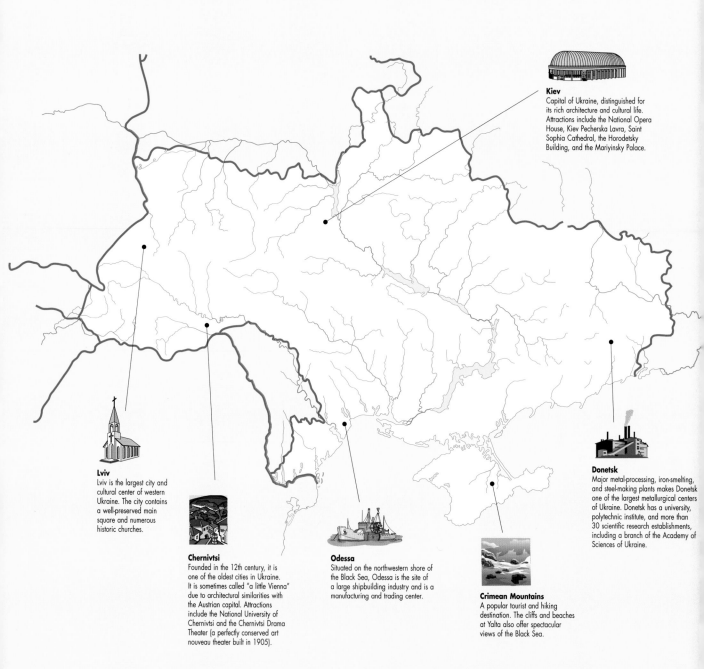

Kiev
Capital of Ukraine, distinguished for its rich architecture and cultural life. Attractions include the National Opera House, Kiev Pecherska Lavra, Saint Sophia Cathedral, the Horodetsky Building, and the Mariyinsky Palace.

Lviv
Lviv is the largest city and cultural center of western Ukraine. The city contains a well-preserved main square and numerous historic churches.

Chernivtsi
Founded in the 12th century, it is one of the oldest cities in Ukraine. It is sometimes called "a little Vienna" due to architectural similarities with the Austrian capital. Attractions include the National University of Chernivtsi and the Chernivtsi Drama Theater (a perfectly conserved art nouveau theater built in 1905).

Odessa
Situated on the northwestern shore of the Black Sea, Odessa is the site of a large shipbuilding industry and is a manufacturing and trading center.

Crimean Mountains
A popular tourist and hiking destination. The cliffs and beaches at Yalta also offer spectacular views of the Black Sea.

Donetsk
Major metal-processing, iron-smelting, and steel-making plants makes Donetsk one of the largest metallurgical centers of Ukraine. Donetsk has a university, polytechnic institute, and more than 30 scientific research establishments, including a branch of the Academy of Sciences of Ukraine.

COUNTRY NAME
Ukraine

CAPITAL CITY
Kiev

FLAG
Two equal horizontal bands of azure (top) and golden yellow, representing grain fields under a blue sky.

OTHER IMPORTANT CITIES
Donetsk, Odessa, Lviv

POPULATION
44.2 million (2016) (This figure includes the population of the Crimea.)

ETHNIC GROUPS
Ukrainians, 77.8 percent; Russians, 17.3 percent; Belarusians, 0.6 percent; Moldovans, 0.5 percent; Crimean Tatars, 0.5 percent; Bulgarians, 0.4 percent; Hungarians, 0.3 percent; Romanians, 0.3 percent; Polish, 0.3 percent, Jews, 0.2 percent; others, 1.8 percent (Note: These statistics are based on the 2001 census, the most recent census as of 2017. The next census is scheduled to take place in 2020. The numbers will differ depending on whether or not Crimea is counted as part of Ukraine or Russia.)

LIFE EXPECTANCY AT BIRTH
Total, 71.8 years
Male, 67.1 years
Female, 76.9 years (2016)

INFANT MORTALITY RATE
8 deaths per 1,000 live births

POPULATION GROWTH RATE
-0.39 percent (2016)

LITERACY RATE
99.8 percent (2015)

RELIGIONS
Ukrainian Orthodox, 66—74 percent; Ukrainian Greek Catholic, 8—10 percent; Protestant/Evangelic, 0.9 percent; Roman Catholic, 0.8 percent; Jewish, >1 percent; Muslim, >1 percent; not religious, 6 percent) (2015)

LANGUAGES
Ukrainian (official), 67 percent; Russian (regional), 29.6 percent; other, 2.9 percent

LEADERS IN POLITICS
Chief of state, President Petro Poroshenko (since June 2014);
Head of government, Prime Minister Volodymyr Groysman (since April 2016)

TIMELINE

IN UKRAINE	IN THE WORLD

911–988 CE
Prince Vladimir of Kiev accepts Byzantine Orthodoxy. Beginning of Russian Christianity.

1000
Icelandic explorer Leif Erikson becomes first European to land in North America.

1237
Mongols conquer Russian lands. Mongols under Batu Khan occupy and destroy Kiev.

1492
Christopher Columbus makes first of four voyages to the Americas.

1620
Pilgrims sail the *Mayflower* to America.

1654
Union of Ukraine and Russia announced.

1709
Peter the Great defeats Charles XII at Poltava in Ukraine, ending the Swedish empire.

1776
US Declaration of Independence

1783
Catherine the Great annexes the Crimea to the Russian Empire.

1789–1799
The French Revolution

1794
Ukraine's port city of Odessa is founded.

1853–1856
The Crimean War.

1861–1865
US Civil War

1869
The Suez Canal opens.

1917–1921
Ukraine declares independence following the collapse of the Russian Empire. The Ukrainian Soviet Socialist Republic is established.

1914–1918
World War I

1932
About 7 million peasants perish in famine during Stalin's collectivization campaign.

1937
Mass executions and deportations as Stalin launches purge against intellectuals.

1939–1945
World War II

1941–1944
Nazi Germany occupies Ukraine.

IN UKRAINE	IN THE WORLD
1945	
Allied victory in World War II leads to Soviet annexation of western Ukrainian lands.	**1966**
	The Chinese Cultural Revolution
	1969
	Apollo 11 mission spaceflight; Neil Armstrong becomes first human on the moon.
1986	
Nuclear power disaster at Chernobyl.	
1991	**1991**
Ukraine declares independence. About 250,000 exiled Crimean Tatars return to Crimea following collapse of Soviet Union.	Breakup of the Soviet Union
	1997
2000	Hong Kong is returned to China.
Chernobyl nuclear power plant is shut down and sealed.	
	2001
2002	Terrorists crash planes in New York, Washington, DC, and Pennsylvania.
Mass protests demanding resignation of President Kuchma, who is accused of corruption and misrule.	
	2003
2004	War in Iraq begins.
Presidential candidate Viktor Yushchenko poisoned prior to election.	
2004–2005	
Orange Revolution demonstrations	
	2008
	US elects first African American president, Barack Obama.
2013–2014	
Ukrainian Revolution (Euromaidan) Security forces kill at least 77 protesters in Kiev. President Yanukovych flees to Russia.	
2014	
Russia seizes, annexes Crimea.	**2015–2016**
	ISIS launches terror attacks in Belgium and France.
2017	**2017**
Fighting between Ukraine and Russia continues on eastern border.	Donald Trump becomes US president.

GLOSSARY

bandura (bahn-DOO-rah)
A multistringed, irregularly-shaped musical instrument.

bohomaz (boh-hoh-MAHZ)
An artist specializing in religious designs.

borscht (BORSH)
A classic Ukrainian soup made with red beets, meat, and other ingredients.

chernozem (cher-noh-ZEM)
Black Ukrainian soil.

hetman (HET-mahn)
The title given to prominent Cossack leaders in the fifteenth to eighteenth centuries.

hopak (hoh-PAHK)
An energetic dance performed by men.

horilka (hoh-RIL-kah)
Ukrainian vodka.

hryvna (HRIV-nah)
The monetary unit (UAH) in Kievan Rus, reintroduced in 1996.

karbovanets (kahr-BOH-vah-nets)
The temporary currency from 1992 to 1996.

kistka (KIST-kah)
The tool used for drawing wax patterns on Easter eggs.

kobzar (kob-ZAHR)
A folk singer or bard.

Kozak (koh-ZAHK)
Cossack, a Ukrainian military man of the fifteenth to eighteenth centuries.

krashanka (KRAH-shahn-kah)
A Ukrainian Easter egg dyed in one bright color.

Lavra (LAH-vrah)
The monastery of the highest importance under the direct jurisdiction of the patriarch of the Ukrainian Orthodox Church.

militsya (mih-LIH-tsiah)
Police.

oblast (OB-lahst)
State or province.

pyrohy (pih-roh-HIH)
Pastries with various fillings, such as meat, vegetables, or sweets.

pysanka (PIH-sahn-kah)
A Ukrainian Easter egg with an artistic multicolored design.

trembita (trem-BEE-tah)
A wind instrument used in the Carpathian Mountains.

varenyki (vah-REH-nih-kih)
Dumplings with various fillings.

FOR FURTHER INFORMATION

BOOKS

Alexievich, Svetlana. *Voices from Chernobyl: The Oral History of a Nuclear Disaster*. New York: Picador, 2006.

Di Duca, Marc, and Leonid Ragozin. *Lonely Planet Ukraine*. Franklin, Tennessee: Lonely Planet, 2014.

Hercules, Olia. *Mamushka: Recipes from Ukraine and Eastern Europe*. San Francisco: Weldon Owen, 2015.

Judah, Tim. *In Wartime: Stories from Ukraine*. New York: Tim Duggan Books, 2015.

Reid, Anna. *Borderland: A Journey Through the History of Ukraine*. New York: Basic Books, 2015.

FILMS

No Place on Earth. Magnolia Pictures, 2013

NOVA: Building Chernobyls' Mega Tomb. PBS, 2017.

Ukraine: From Democracy to Chaos. Journeyman Pictures, 2016.

ONLINE

BBC News. Ukraine country profile. http://www.bbc.com/news/world-europe-18018002

CIA World Factbook, Ukraine. https://www.cia.gov/library/publications/the-world-factbook/geos/up.html

Euromaidan Press. http://euromaidanpress.com

Lonely Planet. Ukraine. https://www.lonelyplanet.com/ukraine

New York Times, The. Ukraine articles and archives. https://www.nytimes.com/topic/destination/ukraine

The Guardian. Ukraine articles and archive. https://www.theguardian.com/world/ukraine

Ukraine Government Portal (in English) http://www.kmu.gov.ua/control/en

BIBLIOGRAPHY

BBC News. "Ukraine crisis in maps." BBC, February 18, 2015. http://www.bbc.com/news/world-europe-27308526

Berga, Alan and Volodymyr Verbyany. "That Boom You Hear Is Ukraine's Agriculture." Bloomberg Businessweek, October 13, 2016. https://www.bloomberg.com/news/articles/2016-10-14/that-boom-you-hear-is-ukraine-s-agriculture

Burridge, Tom. "Chernobyl's legacy 30 years on." BBC News, Ukraine. April 26, 2016. http://www.bbc.com/news/world-europe-36115240

Central Intelligence Agency. CIA World Factbook, Ukraine. https://www.cia.gov/library/publications/the-world-factbook/geos/up.html

Coynash, Halya. "Putin's Bridge to Crimea Is Doomed to Collapse." *Newsweek*, January 13, 2017. http://www.newsweek.com/putin-bridge-crimea-doomed-collapse-541578

Euromaidan Press. http://euromaidanpress.com

Freedom House. https://freedomhouse.org/report/freedom-press/2016/ukraine

Herszenhorn, David M. "Crimea Votes to Secede From Ukraine as Russian Troops Keep Watch." *The New York Times*, March 16, 2014. https://www.nytimes.com/2014/03/17/world/europe/crimea-ukraine-secession-vote-referendum.html

McKenna, Cameron. "Amendments to the Constitution of Ukraine passed: Ukraine takes a major step towards a European System of Justice." Lexology, June 9, 2016. http://www.lexology.com/library/detail.aspx?g=212fa5f8-4f4b-4b4d-9d5a-693579e0c95e

Taylor, Adam. "To understand Crimea, take a look back at its complicated history." *The Washington Post*, February 27, 2014. https://www.washingtonpost.com/news/worldviews/wp/2014/02/27/to-understand-crimea-take-a-look-back-at-its-complicated-history

Visit Kiev Ukraine. "Ukraine Tourism and Visitor Statistics." http://www.visitkievukraine.com/essential/tourism-statistics

World Jewish Congress. Ukraine. http://www.worldjewishcongress.org/en/about/communities/UA

Yashin, Ilya. "Russia's gradual swallowing of Ukraine." *The Washington Times*. February 8, 2017. http://www.washingtontimes.com/news/2017/feb/8/russia-taking-over-ukraine-must-be-guarded-against

Yekelchyk, Serhy. The Ukrainian Crisis: In Russia's Long Shadow. *Origins*, vol. 7, issue 9, June 2014. http://origins.osu.edu/article/ukrainian-crisis-russias-long-shadow

INDEX

INDEX